MARTIN LUTHER
KING JR.

CHRISTINE HATT

WORLD ALMANAC® LIBRARY

Please visit our web site at: www.worldalmanaclibrary.com
For a free color catalog describing World Almanac® Library's list
of high-quality books and multimedia programs, call 1-800-848-2928 (USA)
or 1-800-387-3178 (Canada). World Almanac® Library's fax: (414) 332-3567.

Library of Congress Cataloging-in-Publication Data

Hatt, Christine.
    Martin Luther King Jr. / by Christine Hatt.
       p. cm. — (Judge for yourself)
    Includes bibliographical references and index.
    ISBN 0-8368-5562-0 (lib. bdg.)
      1. King, Martin Luther, Jr., 1929-1968—Juvenile literature. 2. African Americans—
Biography—Juvenile literature. 3. Civil rights workers—United States—Biography—
Juvenile literature. 4. Baptists—United States—Clergy—Biography—Juvenile literature.
5. African Americans—Civil rights—History—20th century—Juvenile literature. I. Title.
II. Series.
    E185.97.K5H36   2004
    323'.092—dc22
    [B]   2003060945

This North American edition first published in 2004 by
World Almanac® Library
330 West Olive Street, Suite 100
Milwaukee, WI 53212 USA

This U.S. edition copyright © 2004 by World Almanac® Library. Original edition published in Great Britain by
Evans Brothers Limited. Copyright © 2002 by Evans Brothers Limited, 2A Portman Mansions, Chiltern Street,
London W1U 6NR, United Kingdom. This U.S. edition published under license from Evans Brothers Limited.

Consultant: Dr. John A. Kirk, Royal Holloway College, University of London
Editor: Jinny Johnson
Design: Mark Holt
Maps: Tim Smith
Production: Jenny Mulvanny
Picture research: Julia Bird
Gareth Stevens editor: Alan Wachtel
Gareth Stevens designer: Scott M. Krall

Photo credits: t–top, c–center, b–bottom, r–right, l–left, Corbis: Front cover (top), back cover (center), title
page, 4, 12, 15, 19, 20, 22, 23, 26b, 27, 33, 34r, 35b, 37, 41b, 42, 43, 46, 49, 53b, 57; Hulton Getty: 5l, 5r, 6t, 7,
10b, 10t, 11b, 13, 14, 16, 17b, 18, 24, 25, 28, 34l, 35t, 36, 39, 44, 47, 53t, 54, 55, 56; J. S. Library International:
8; Mary Evans Picture Library: 9, 11t, 17t; Topham Picturepoint: Front cover (main image and bottom), Back
cover (top and bottom), 21, 26t, 29, 31, 32, 38, 41t, 45, 48, 52, 58, 59b, 59t, 60, 61

Printed in Canada

1 2 3 4 5 6 7 8 9 08 07 06 05 04

CONTENTS

INTRODUCTION

The Baptist preacher and political activist Dr. Martin Luther King Jr. lived for fewer than 40 years, but in that short time, he transformed the lives of black Americans. As a result of the nonviolent campaigns he and others led in the United States during the 1950s and 1960s, black people gained not only recognition of their civil rights but also a new sense of self-esteem following the era of segregation.

This book looks at Martin Luther King Jr. and his activities in two different ways. In the first part, you can read the straightforward story of his life, from his birth as a preacher's son in Atlanta, Georgia, in 1929 to his tragic assassination in Memphis, Tennessee, in 1968. This part is divided into chapters, and

King (center, next to his wife Coretta) leads a major civil rights march through Selma, Alabama, in March 1965.

it also includes special features that highlight two subjects, slavery in the United States until its abolition in 1865 and the Jim Crow era in the South that followed abolition.

In the second part of the book, you can examine the main themes of King's life—for example, his belief in nonviolent protest, his struggle for black civil rights, and his opposition to the Vietnam War—more closely. To help you assess King's ideals and actions for yourself, this part is divided into sections, each headed with an important question to consider. The first two pages in each section provide one possible answer, together with quotations, statistics, and other facts to back it up. The next two pages provide a second potential answer, also with supporting evidence and information.

The question pages can be used in several ways. You may just want to read them through, look at both answers and their sup-

CHANGING NAMES

During Martin Luther King's lifetime, black Americans were generally known as either "colored" people or as Negroes. During the mid-1960s, as the Black Power movement rose to prominence, the term "Afro-American" became more popular, especially among black people themselves. Today, "African American" is widely used by members of all communities. To avoid any possible confusion, this book uses the more general term "black" throughout. (Racists have used many derogatory terms to refer to blacks. Where these words appear in this book, they are clearly attributed to the person who used them.)

porting evidence, and then make up your own mind about which answer is stronger. Perhaps you could also write down the reasons for your decision. Alternatively, the material can be used for a classroom debate between two groups, each arguing for a different answer. The sources may also inspire further research. You may wish to use the library or the Internet to find more data to back your answers to the questions on which these pages focus.

The question pages have another purpose. They are designed to show you that facts and statistics can be used to support completely different points of view. This is why historians have to sift through a great deal of material from a wide variety of sources before they can reach reliable conclusions about the past. Even then, answers are rarely clear-cut and may be overturned by new evidence. As you consider the questions, remember that neither of the answers provided may be completely correct. Using all the information in both parts of the book—and any more that you can find—it is up to you to judge for yourself.

Racial tension often led to unrest even in northern cities. This man was wounded in a riot in Newark, New Jersey, in 1967.

During the Jim Crow era in the South, blacks and whites were not allowed to use the same public water coolers.

CHAPTER ONE

EARLY LIFE

Martin Luther King Jr. was born on January 15, 1929, in Atlanta, Georgia. At first, he was called Michael, after his father, but in 1934, Michael Sr. changed both his own and his son's name to Martin Luther, after the 16th-century German leader of the Protestant Reformation. As a child, however, Martin Luther King Jr. was usually known affectionately as M.L.

German priest Martin Luther (1483–1546) was a founder of Protestant Christianity.

FAMILY RELATIONSHIPS

Although M.L. grew up in a secure and loving family, there were some tensions. His strong-willed father dominated the household. The child of poor sharecroppers, Martin Sr. had struggled for his education and to become pastor of Atlanta's Ebenezer Baptist Church. He intended to ensure that M.L., his older sister Christine and his younger brother Alfred Daniel (also known as A.D.) had a smoother path through life. He demanded good behavior and hard work. Like many parents of the time, he beat his children if he felt they had done wrong.

Two women also shaped M.L.'s early years. The first was his mother, Alberta, whose father had been the previous pastor of Ebenezer Church. She was a quiet, gentle person who lived in her husband's shadow. The second was his maternal grandmother, a warmer, much more exuberant woman, to whom M.L. felt a special closeness.

M.L.'s belief in God was nurtured not only by his father and other close relatives, but also by the wider "family" he encountered in church every Sunday. In church, some 4,000 members of Atlanta's black community found refuge from the mistreatment that was their daily experience in a state where segregation laws were strictly enforced. During the sermons by Martin Sr., the congregation cried aloud in response, releasing all their pent-up anger and sorrow.

STARTING SCHOOL

During his preschool years, M.L. moved between two

places of security—his comfortable home, which stood in the black middle-class neighborhood of Sweet Auburn, and his father's church. Although the Great Depression hit the United States in the 1930s, plunging millions into poverty, Martin Sr.'s financial prudence and job as a pastor ensured that the King family never became poor. When M.L. began school in 1935, however, the harsh realities of life as a black person in the United States began to hit home.

His first shock came on the very day that he started at Yonge Street Elementary School. His best friend, a white boy, was beginning his education at the same time. M.L. found that his playmate was not attending the same school as him and neither were any other white children. Wanting to find out why, he stopped at his friend's house on the way

As a grown man and a minister himself, Martin Luther King Jr. (far left) listens to his father preach at Ebenezer Baptist Church in 1964, just as he did when he was a boy.

home. His friend's parents informed him that the two boys were no longer allowed to play together because their son was white and M.L. was "colored."

M.L. rushed back to his own house to discuss this troubling development. His parents now realized it was impossible to shield him from the truth anymore. That evening, they explained the history of black people in the United States to their son. As M.L. heard about the horrors of slavery, the dashed hopes that followed abolition in 1865, and the Jim Crow laws that still were enforced in the South, his childhood world fell apart. In response, his parents urged him to be strong and be proud of his ancestry, saying, "You must always feel that you are *somebody*."

GROWING UP

After leaving Yonge Street, M.L. continued his education at David T. Howard Colored Elementary School. Bright, hard-working, and popular, he was nevertheless called a "shrimp" because he was short for his age.

The movie *Gone with the Wind* premiered in Atlanta in 1939, when King was ten. It portrays a romantic view of 19th-century life in the South from a white viewpoint.

The success and acceptance M.L. found at school, church, and home were not matched by his experience in the wider world. Almost every day, he noticed another way in which he and other black people were treated as second class. They had to sit in the back of buses, away from white passengers. They were refused service at the best restaurants and given the worst seats at the movies. They were even required to use separate public toilets. In addition, white people often spoke to them in an offensive manner, calling them "niggers" and addressing grown men as "boy."

In December 1941, Japan attacked the American naval base in Pearl Harbor, Hawaii, and President Franklin D. Roosevelt led the United States into World War II. The following year, M.L. began attending Booker T. Washington High School. Now 13, he was starting to exhibit the usual anxieties and rebelliousness of adolescence. For him, they had a particular intensity. The injustice of racism preyed on his mind, provoking a bitter anger. In addition, his relationship with his domineering father was growing difficult.

MOREHOUSE COLLEGE

When he was just 15, M.L. won a place at Atlanta's prestigious, all-black Morehouse College—three years earlier than was normal. At first, he struggled academically at the college. This was partly because of his age and partly because the education he had received at his previous schools was poor. Despite his obvious abilities, he had a lower reading level than most of his classmates. Rage at a system that considered black children too unimportant to educate properly drove M.L. to catch up. Although he was never a top student at Morehouse, his teachers saw him as a sharp thinker and an excellent speaker. M.L. was also developing in another way. He had discovered women and was soon stepping out with a string of girlfriends.

FINDING A VOCATION

Unlike many other Morehouse students, M.L. lived at home, and during this period, his complex relationship with his father came under even greater strain. M.L. loved Martin Sr. greatly, but he was also resentful of his father's stubborn belief that he was always right. There were many clashes over minor issues. Martin Jr. loved dancing, for example, but his father thought it sinful. The growing religious differences between them, however, were much harder to resolve.

Martin Sr. was a fundamentalist. That is, he believed in the complete and literal truth of the Bible. The more Martin Jr. studied and reflected, the more convinced he became that this simply could not be so. Thoughts of following in his father's footsteps as a preacher were now replaced by plans to become a lawyer who would fight against injustice through the courts. Two instructors at Morehouse, however, showed Martin Jr. (he had stopped, by this time, using the nickname M.L.) that there was another way.

These two men were the college principal, Dr. Benjamin E. Mays, and the director of

Morehouse's School of Religion, George D. Kelsey, who taught the young scholar to interpret the Bible. Mays and Kelsey also showed him how relevant the Biblical stories of struggle and salvation were to black people in the United States. Martin Jr. saw that he could be a minister of the Gospel while working to bring his people justice in the here and now. There was no need to copy his father's style of preaching or to accept his theology. Martin Jr. found he could serve God in his own way.

ORDINATION AND AFTER

Martin Sr. was delighted by his son's decision but wanted to test Martin Jr.'s calling to make sure it was real. In 1947, he arranged for the 18-year-old to preach a sermon at Ebenezer Baptist Church. The teenager's arguments were lofty, and his preaching was more sober than his father's. There was no mistaking, however, his conviction and power.

Martin Jr.'s performance was good enough to satisfy his father. It was with great pride that Martin Sr. ordained his son as a Baptist preacher on February 25, 1948, and made him assistant pastor at Ebenezer Baptist Church. In the spring, Martin Jr. graduated from Morehouse and began to plan his future. All he knew for sure was that he intended to engage in the struggle for racial justice not quietly from the sidelines but in "the very heat of it."

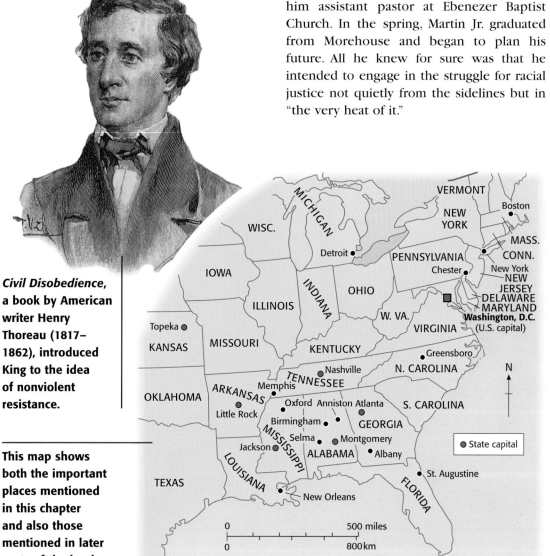

Civil Disobedience, **a book by American writer Henry Thoreau (1817– 1862), introduced King to the idea of nonviolent resistance.**

This map shows both the important places mentioned in this chapter and also those mentioned in later parts of the book.

SLAVERY

A Dutch sea captain brought the first black people to North America in 1619 and sold these 20 men to white Virginia settlers. It was not until the 1680s, when serious labor shortages developed, that the transport of black people across the Atlantic from Africa greatly increased. At first, many blacks were treated no worse than poor white servants. As the black population grew, however, so did racism. By 1700, the white community had enslaved most blacks in North America, denying them even the most basic rights.

THE SLAVE TRADE

As the demand for labor steadily grew in 18th-century North America—especially on the plantations of the South—the slave trade flourished. Europeans took growing numbers of African blacks prisoner, chaining them below deck in cramped, filthy ships, in which disease spread rapidly. Many did not survive the transatlantic journey. By the time slaving trips ended, about 600,000 Africans had been brought to North America. Among them were the great-grandparents of Martin Luther King.

A scene in a slave ship traveling from Africa to the Americas.

BIRTH OF THE UNITED STATES

In the late 18th century, the 13 British colonies of North America rebelled against the British government and war broke out. The 1776 Declaration of Independence that announced the founding of the United States boldly proclaimed: "We hold these truths to be self-evident: That all men are created equal. . . ." Efforts to apply this noble principle to blacks as well as whites by abolishing the slave trade, however, did not succeed. In fact, as a result of the Southern plantation owners' insistence, the

American statesmen sign the Declaration of Independence in 1776.

1787 United States Constitution stipulated that the slave trade could not be banned before 1808.

NORTH VS. SOUTH

The abolition of slavery itself was another matter. In the North, moral arguments and economic realities—the region was industrializing rapidly, so fewer farm laborers were needed—led to the outlawing of slavery in state after state. In the South, however, the cotton industry was expanding (particularly after the invention in 1793 of the cotton gin), fueling demand for workers. After the abolition of the slave trade in 1808, planters met this need by buying slaves from other slave owners.

The cotton gin separated cotton seeds from the fibers used to make cloth.

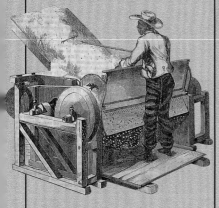

ABRAHAM LINCOLN AND THE CIVIL WAR

In the mid-19th century, the differences between North and South became greater. The United States was expanding west and there were long debates in Congress about whether new territories should permit or ban slavery. In 1854, the Republican Party was founded in the North to oppose the spread of slavery. Six years later, Republican Abraham Lincoln was elected president. This development prompted seven (later eleven) states in the South to secede and form the Confederacy. On April 12, 1861, forces of the Confederacy began a war against the Union forces of the North.

THE EMANCIPATION PROCLAMATION

At the outset of the Civil War, Lincoln's aim was to bring the Confederate states back into the Union. The conflict, however, lasted far longer than the president expected. In 1862, he decided to threaten the South's economic survival by proclaiming that if the Confederacy did not surrender within 100 days, he would free all slaves in its territories. As there was no response, Lincoln issued the Emancipation Proclamation on January 1, 1863. It stated that these slaves were ". . . then, thence-forward, and forever free," making the abolition of slavery in the Confederate areas a second goal.

ABOLITION AND AFTER

In January 1865, as the Civil War was drawing to a close, President Lincoln steered an even more important antislavery measure through Congress. The historic Thirteenth Amendment to the Constitution abolished slavery throughout the United States. On April 9, 1865, the Civil War ended with the surrender of the Confederate forces. It seemed that black Americans in both the North and South could reasonably hope for a better future. In fact, their struggle had just begun.

President Abraham Lincoln

SLAVE LIFE

Most slaves in the United States labored in fields, either on the rice and cotton plantations of the South or on tobacco and other farms farther north. Because their work week usually lasted for six long days, sunrise to sunset, they had little time for rest. Slaves in domestic service, many of them women, did not face the same physical demands as farm workers, but they often had to deal with ill-tempered, spiteful mistresses and sexual approaches from masters. In addition, they were expected to work seven days a week.

Even when not working, slaves were treated with casual cruelty. Legally, they were simply a type of property that their masters could buy and sell at will. Slave-traders did not hesitate to split up families if it suited them, sometimes handing a mother over to one planter and her children to another. Punishments, from a simple reprimand to a severe whipping, were meted out for even minor misdemeanors. Masters generally provided their slaves with adequate food and housing but little or no education. The vast majority of slaves were illiterate.

In the face of such constant abuse, slaves struggled to maintain their dignity and self-esteem. They worked toward this goal by building strong extended families and by establishing networks of churches. In these churches, they could worship in their own way and draw comfort from Biblical texts that speak of each individual's worth in the eyes of God and of the glories that awaited in heaven. It was this powerful religious tradition that Martin Luther King Jr. inherited.

COLLEGE YEARS

Once Martin Jr.'s Morehouse years were over, his father hoped he would settle down. What better future could there be than to marry his regular girlfriend, start a family, and eventually become chief pastor at Ebenezer Baptist? But Martin Jr. wanted instead to study at Crozer Seminary, a theological college in Pennsylvania. As he was now a mature 19-year-old, his father decided not to stand in his way.

STARTING COLLEGE

Martin Jr. arrived in Chester, the town where Crozer was located, in the fall of 1948. Full of intellectual curiosity, he was determined not to waste this opportunity to learn. As one of only six young blacks in a college with a student body of almost 100 students, King was also eager to prove himself.

From the beginning, King studied hard, arriving at classes on time and spending long hours at his desk. He was wary of showing his more fun-loving side, because he had no wish to confirm the white stereotype of black men as jokers who never buckled down to serious work. Just as he was starting to relax, an event occurred that highlighted the hatred some white students felt for Crozer's small black minority.

Among King's fellow students was a young white man from North Carolina who believed that black people should not be allowed to attend the college. One day, while he was still a freshman, that student returned to his room to find all his belongings in disarray. This was not an unusual event. At Crozer, there was a hazing tradition of "raiding"—that is, completely ransacking—the rooms of new students.

Despite a total lack of evidence, the North Carolinian decided this prank was a malicious attack and that King was to blame.

The grand buildings of Crozer Seminary in Chester, Pennsylvania, where Martin Luther King studied theology from 1948 to 1951.

This 1930 picture shows Gandhi (the bald figure with bowed head) leading supporters on a march against a British tax on salt.

He crashed into King's room shouting racist abuse and threatening to kill his fellow student with the gun he was holding. King responded with magnificent calm, simply denying responsibility for the raid. Luckily, three other students arrived and persuaded the angry student to drop his weapon.

The incident was soon reported to Crozer's student council, with the expectation that the angry white student would be dismissed from the college. King, however, refused to press charges, saying he was content with the apology his attacker had offered him. His restraint won him many friends—including the man who had threatened to shoot him.

SEMINARY STUDIES

As the months passed, King filled his head with new learning, from academic Christian theology to the ideas of secular philosophers both ancient and modern. Of special interest were the writings of Walter Rauschenbusch, a white Baptist preacher who had worked in the slums of late 19th-century New York. His book *Christianity and the Social Crisis* argued that Christians had a duty to tackle the poor's economic and social problems. It was not right to offer hope only for the afterlife. The Kingdom of God that Jesus preached had to be established on Earth.

King also became enthralled by the work of Mahatma Gandhi. Earlier in the 20th century, this Indian leader had mobilized the poverty-stricken masses of his country to fight against British colonial rule. They had done so successfully—India won its independence in 1947—mainly by using the demonstrations, boycotts, and other techniques of nonviolent resistance that Gandhi had advocated.

For King, this was an "electrifying" revelation. He wanted to help American blacks win their freedom, not from foreign rule but from injustice. As a Christian, he had grave doubts about using violence for this purpose, but the pacifist alternative seemed a feeble means of confronting such a profound problem. Gandhi's tactics offered a third possibility. Gandhi's tactics were known in Hindi as *satyagraha*, or "truth force." King later became convinced that this active force, not simply the passive absence of violence, was the way to defeat the world's evil.

PREACHING PRACTICE

Despite the fact that it was integrated, Crozer was an essentially white environment. In all his time there, King never forgot his roots in the black church. These roots were strengthened immeasurably by regular visits to nearby "Barbour University." "Barbour University" was not an academic institution but the home of J. Pius Barbour, who was a distinguished pastor, a friend of King's father, and Crozer's first black graduate.

It was at Barbour's house that King refined his natural preaching abilities and learned to combine the raw power, emotion, and faith of traditional black sermons with the more intellectual Crozer approach. By observing Barbour at work, he also discovered how to incorporate ideas about economics and politics into more obviously "religious" addresses and how to discuss the complex notions of great thinkers without losing the attention of his audience. By the end of this training, King's oratory was able to captivate black and white listeners alike.

FROM CROZER TO BOSTON

King's time at Crozer ended in June 1951, when he graduated first in his class with a B.A. in Divinity. The seminary prize for this achievement was a $1,300 scholarship to attend any place of postgraduate study that he chose. After spending the summer in Atlanta, the 22-year-old headed north to begin work on his Ph.D. at Boston University.

INTEGRATING THE ARMED FORCES

During World War II, about one million black Americans served in the armed forces. They had not done so, however, on the same terms as whites. In the army, black units were fully segregated and usually under the command of white officers. The navy was integrated, but blacks did not have the right to hold leadership roles. Black airmen served only in a specially established corps that trained at Tuskegee Airfield, in Alabama (below).

In April 1945, as the war was drawing to a close, Democrat Harry S. Truman was elected president. Over the next seven years, he made great efforts to force the issue of black civil rights onto the national agenda. His proposed antidiscrimination laws failed to survive Congress, thanks to the bitter opposition of members from the South, but Truman was able to make one significant change without congressional approval. In 1948, the president issued Executive Order 9981, which started the process of desegregating the U.S. armed forces. By the mid-1950s, the army, air force, and navy were all integrated.

King's father indicated his approval by giving his son an eye-catching green Chevrolet car.

Once in Boston, King began to study Christianity in even greater depth than before and learn about a wide range of other subjects, from Islam to psychology. As usual, he thought deeply about each new topic, trying to see whether it had any relevance to his own life and beliefs. By spring 1953, he had completed all of his coursework and decided to remain at the same university to write his Ph.D thesis.

LOVE AND MARRIAGE

It was by no means all work and no play in Boston. King often spent time at the Totem Pole jazz club. He also dined at restaurants where generous platefuls of fried chicken and other kinds of southern "soul food" were served. But there was for many months no serious girlfriend in his life.

Finally, early in 1952, King decided that the time had come to find a lifelong partner. He asked a friend, Mary Powell, if she knew of anyone suitable. Mrs. Powell suggested Coretta Scott, a young woman from Marion, Alabama, who was studying to be a singer at the New England Conservatory of Music. The same evening, King telephoned Coretta and arranged to meet her for lunch the next day.

King liked Coretta at once. She was pretty and bright, with a quiet inner strength. Coretta did not feel the same immediate attraction to King. He was short and very intense, questioning her about politics and other serious issues that most men would not even have mentioned on a first date. In any case, she was not a regular churchgoer and thought that preachers were dull. But he slowly won her over. At the end of the date, King shocked Coretta by telling her that she would make an ideal wife.

From then on, King saw Coretta regularly, but she was reluctant to marry. She simply could not imagine herself as the demure, ever-smiling wife of a preacher. She also

Martin and and his wife Coretta during their early years together. They were married in 1953.

knew that taking on such a role would mean giving up her dreams of a career. There would not be time to help her husband with church business, raise a family, and be a professional singer. In the end, King got his way. The couple wed on June 18, 1953, in the garden of Coretta's parents' house in Marion. After a brief honeymoon, the couple returned to Boston to complete their studies.

JIM CROW

"Jim Crow" was a black character in a song-and-dance act performed by American entertainer Thomas Rice. From the late 19th century, the term "Jim Crow" was used as a name for the system of racial segregation and the related laws that grew up in the South after the United States Civil War. Martin Luther King Jr. dedicated his life to fighting Jim Crow.

INTRODUCING JIM CROW

After Reconstruction ended, the southern states slowly but surely put up roadblocks to civil rights for black people. First, they introduced measures to prevent blacks from voting, including poll taxes, literacy tests, and grandfather clauses. Next, they began to pass laws enforcing segregation in public buildings and public transportation.

Black people also suffered from persecution by the Ku Klux Klan, a white supremacist organization founded in 1866. The first aim of this organization was to stop black people from voting

In 1892, black carpenter Homer A. Plessy decided to challenge one of the segregation laws in Louisiana. Plessy sat in a "whites-

Members of the Ku Klux Klan, a white supremacist organization.

only" train carriage and let himself be arrested. The Supreme Court made the historic *Plessy* v. *Ferguson* ruling on the case in 1896. It stated that Louisiana segregation laws did not violate the Fourteenth Amendment, as facilities for blacks were "separate but equal." After the ruling, more segregation laws were passed and the Jim Crow era began in earnest. Black facilities were rarely equal, but the courts did not intervene.

FIGHTING BACK

Black people soon began to fight back. Among the first campaigners for better treatment was ex-slave Booker T. Washington, who became the first principal of the Tuskegee Institute in Alabama, an industrial and agricultural college for black

RECONSTRUCTION

Reconstruction began in 1865, after the Civil War ended. During this period, the southern states recovered from the fighting and rejoined the Union. At the same time, southern state governments tried to limit the rights of former slaves, while the federal government was trying to increase them. In 1866, Congress passed the Civil Rights Act, which gave blacks "full and equal benefit" of all laws relating to themselves and their property. After imposing military rule in the South in 1867, Congress also passed the Fourteenth and Fifteenth Amendments to the Constitution. Blacks were elected to state governments, strengthening black rights.

In the 1870s, intimidation of black voters and a white backlash allowed Democratic Party members who opposed racial equality to regain control of most southern governments. The situation became worse for blacks after the 1876 presidential election. The result was disputed, and southern white Democrats would accept the victory of Republican candidate Rutherford B. Hayes only if they were given the right to rule in the South without further federal interference. In 1877, the last federal troops left the region, and Reconstruction ended.

THE FOURTEENTH AMENDMENT
(Adopted 1868)
Section 1: All persons born or naturalized in the United States . . . are citizens of the United States and of the State wherein they reside. No State shall make or enforce any law which shall abridge the privileges or immunities of citizens of the United States. . . .

THE FIFTEENTH AMENDMENT
(Adopted 1870)
Section 1: The right of citizens of the United States to vote shall not be denied or abridged by the United States or by any State on account of race, color, or previous condition of servitude.

students. Washington advised blacks not to protest against political inequality but to educate themselves for manual jobs. In this way, he thought, they would slowly improve their place in society. For many black people, this simply was not enough.

A more radical approach was adopted by black sociologist W.E.B. DuBois. In 1905, DuBois arranged a meeting of like-minded people near Niagara Falls. There they founded the Niagara Movement, whose aim was to win equal civil rights for blacks. The movement achieved little, but five years later, a more effective organization, the National Association for the Advancement of Colored People (NAACP), was formed. DuBois served as its publicity director and edited its journal, *The Crisis*.

NAACP strategy was to take to court any state government that it believed was violating the Fourteenth- and Fifteenth-Amendment rights of black people. Among its first victories was the 1915 *Guinn* v. *United States* ruling, which outlawed Oklahoma's grandfather clause. Another organization often supported the NAACP in its legal battles. This was

American educator Booker T. Washington was born a slave.

the National Urban League (NUL), founded in 1911. The aim of this organization was to help the many southern blacks who migrated to northern cities looking for work, especially during World War I and the Depression era.

WORLD WAR II AND AFTER

During World War II, thousands more black people moved north to work in factories. They won an important legal victory in June 1941, when President Franklin D. Roosevelt issued an Executive Order establishing the Fair Employment Practices Committee (FEPC) and outlawing discrimination in the defense industries. Blacks in the armed forces, however, faced prejudice and, in the army and air force, segregation.

In 1942, black people set up a new civil rights organization, the Congress of Racial Equality (CORE). Founded in Chicago, CORE's main aim was to organize protests against segregation in the northern cities of the United States.

In 1945, after World War II ended, the NAACP, the NUL, and CORE all continued their work. It was a case brought by the NAACP that led to the historic *Brown* v. *Board of Education of Topeka* ruling in 1954. This ruling overturned the *Plessy* v. *Ferguson* decision and opened the way for Martin Luther King Jr.'s new challenge to Jim Crow.

National Guardsmen patrol Chicago streets during a 1919 race riot.

MINISTRY IN MONTGOMERY

Soon after his marriage, King decided that he wanted to take on a paying job while continuing to write his Ph.D. thesis on his own time. He was unsure whether to seek work as a college lecturer, as several of his teachers urged him to do, or to fulfill his father's dream and become a full-time Baptist preacher. Eventually, he made up his mind. He would serve as a preacher first and return to academic life later in his career.

THE MOVE TO MONTGOMERY

Early in 1954, King made his way to Montgomery, the capital of Alabama, to preach a trial sermon at Dexter Avenue Baptist Church. It was the best-known place of black Christian worship in the city, and its congregation wanted a chance to see whether this young man fresh from college would make a suitable pastor.

The 25-year-old King was nervous. Dexter's middle-class parishioners were famous for letting a man know if his sermons were not up to scratch. In his trial sermon, King simply entrusted himself to God and let his incomparable voice soar out over the pews, speaking about the importance of leading a balanced, loving, Christian life. King's fears proved groundless. At the end of the sermon, a church deacon spoke for the whole congregation when he declared: "That did it!"

In March of the same year, King was formally offered the job as Dexter's pastor, but his pleasure at the offer was combined with anxiety. He and Coretta had grown used to life in the North, and the thought of returning to the segregated South was not appealing. On the other hand, both had families in the region who would provide support, and King felt that it was his Christian duty to serve the

King outside Dexter Avenue Church. The Alabama State Capitol is visible behind him.

18

BROWN v. BOARD OF EDUCATION OF TOPEKA

In 1954, the parents of a black girl named Linda Brown, backed by the NAACP, took the Board of Education of Topeka, Kansas, to court. They claimed that Topeka had no right to enforce school segregation because the practice violated the Fourteenth Amendment to the Constitution. The Supreme Court agreed, with Chief Justice Earl Warren declaring that "separate educational facilities are inherently unequal" and that they were likely to produce "a feeling of inferiority" in black pupils. Every state was obliged, therefore, to desegregate its schools. The Court did not draw up a timetable for change, simply stating, in 1955, that desegregation should go ahead "with all deliberate speed." Ten years later, fewer than 25 percent of southern school districts had complied.

black community where the need was greatest. It was a hard decision, but he began work at Dexter in May 1954 and was officially installed on December 31.

King's new life tested him from the outset. As well as busying himself with the usual tasks of a Christian minister—sermon-writing, religious teaching, and pastoral care of parishioners—he was also active in the local chapter of the NAACP. He also worked on his Ph.D. thesis. The only way to get everything done was to get up at 5:30 A.M. every day.

GROWING TENSIONS

Out in the wider world, developments were taking place that would soon lead to far greater demands on King's time. In a 1954 test case, the U.S. Supreme Court ruled that

The large, airy interior of Dexter Avenue Baptist Church in Montgomery, Alabama. The church is still a thriving place of worship today.

segregated schooling was wrong and should be ended. Predictably, this judgment caused outrage throughout the South. Montgomery's 70,000 whites were used to keeping the city's 50,000 blacks apart from themselves. They established a White Citizens' Council to fight tooth and nail against desegregation and any other moves attempting to improve the status of the black population.

Throughout 1955, King felt the growing tension. Nonetheless, he continued his daily work and family life largely as normal. For him, the year up to December had two highlights. In June, he was awarded his Ph.D., and in November, Yolanda, his first child, was born. Known fondly as Yoki, she brought great joy to both her parents.

ROSA PARKS

Rosa Parks was a black woman employed as a seamstress in a Montgomery store. She was also an active member of the local NAACP. On

Coretta King with all four of her children in 1964. Yoki is standing on the far right, next to her brother, Marty.

December 1, 1955, she worked hard all day and then went Christmas shopping. On the bus ride home, she sat in the black section at the back, glad to rest her aching feet. An incident then occurred that was to alter the course of the black civil rights movement in the United States. When a white man got on the now full bus, Mrs. Parks refused to give up her seat so that he could sit down.

Rosa Parks's action was against Montgomery law, and she was arrested. Once at the police station, she phoned Edward D. Nixon, a forceful NAACP official who had long sought a chance to take the city government to court about its discriminatory bus regulations. This episode seemed to be the answer to his prayers. He rushed to the station to get Mrs. Parks out on bail and then carefully began to make his plans.

THE BUS BOYCOTT

The next morning, Friday, December 2, Nixon phoned King. He explained the situation and asked the young minister to support his idea of a bus boycott. If they could persuade Montgomery's black people not to use the city buses, Nixon argued, they could make a nonviolent stand against the treatment of Rosa Parks and discrimination in general. King agreed and offered to hold a meeting of local black leaders at his church that night. There, they would be able to discuss exactly how to proceed.

The meeting was held, plans were made, and 40,000 publicity leaflets printed and distributed. On Sunday, black preachers across the city announced to their congregations that a bus boycott would begin the next day. After all the preparations were over, Nixon, King, and fellow activists including Ralph Abernathy, the minister of Montgomery's First Baptist Church, could only wait for the morning. Would the black community respond to their call?

To their great relief, the boycott was almost total. On that Monday, Montgomery's blacks

Rosa Lee Parks with her attorney, Charles D. Langford, in 1955, after she was arrested for not giving her seat on a bus to a white man.

made their way to work, school, and college on foot, by taxi, or in any other way that did not involve riding a bus. In court the same day, Rosa Parks was found guilty and fined the sum of fourteen dollars.

THE MONTGOMERY IMPROVEMENT ASSOCIATION

Change was in the air and the black community was ready to act, but it needed clear direction. On the afternoon of December 2, King, Abernathy, Nixon, and others met to discuss the right way forward. They decided to set up a body called the Montgomery Improvement Association (MIA). This group would continue to lead the boycott and campaign more generally against racial discrimination. To his surprise, King was elected president. He was flattered, but wondered how he would deal with this extra burden.

After telling Coretta what had happened, King rushed out again to address an evening meeting at Holt Street Baptist Church. As both people in the overflowing sanctuary and television cameras looked on, King made his first televised speech. He spoke of the plight of blacks, saying, "You know my friends there comes a time when people get *tired* of being trampled over by the iron feet of oppression." He spoke of their right to protest for the equality guaranteed them by the Constitution, and he affirmed that they must protest as Christians, with love and without violence.

The crowd greeted these words with heartfelt cheers and applause, and King firmly believed God had spoken through him that night. While King recovered, shaking from his efforts, Abernathy dealt with the down-to-earth business. The boycott, he announced, would continue until passengers, whatever their color, were allowed to sit down on a first-come, first-served basis; until the abuse of black passengers ended; and until some black bus drivers were hired.

CONTINUING THE STRUGGLE

These demands were extremely moderate. The MIA was not even asking for an end to bus segregation. The city authorities and bus company lawyers, however, refused to budge. They were sure the boycott would soon fizzle out. But they were wrong. Day after day, thousands of Montgomery's blacks trudged to their destinations. Others used the car pool set up by the MIA. This involved making their way to pick-up points where volunteer drivers picked them up and took them to work. When it was time to go home, the operation was carried out in reverse.

As 1956 arrived and the boycott continued, city leaders began to work actively against the MIA. They made it hard for the car pool to operate by refusing to renew insurance on its vehicles. They also arrested pool drivers for minor traffic offenses and canceled their licenses. King was arrested for driving just over the speed limit. The usual punishment would have been a fine, but he was jailed in the police station. He was released after a crowd demonstrated outside.

UNDER THREAT

King and his family soon had to face far worse. They regularly received abusive letters and telephone calls but were usually able to ignore them. One particular call in January was especially chilling. The caller told King to leave Montgomery within three days or "we gonna blow your brains out and blow up

The white backlash against the 1954 Supreme Court ruling was severe. In Mississippi, 14-year-old Emmet Till, a summer visitor from Chicago, was murdered for speaking to a white woman.

your house." King's first instinct was to do as the caller asked. How could he risk the lives of his wife and daughter? Then, however, he felt as never before the sense that Jesus was with him, urging him onward, and there could be no turning back.

The caller's message was not an idle threat. On January 30, while King was at a meeting, a bomb exploded on his house porch. Once he heard the news, he rushed home to see if Coretta and Yoki were all right. To his relief they were unharmed, although deeply shocked. Struggling against his anger, King resolved again to continue the fight.

THE MIRACLE OF MONTGOMERY

The boycott dragged on through 1956, and many blacks, including King, were arrested for participating. Behind the scenes, however, the MIA was making progress. In February, it had made an appeal to the federal courts, claiming that bus segregation violated the Fourteenth Amendment to the Constitution. MIA's hope was that, although the Alabama courts had continually denied blacks justice, the federal system would rule in its favor.

For much of the year, as the legal wrangling continued, King toured the United States. In this way, he won publicity for his cause and both dear friends and bitter enemies for himself. By the fall, when he returned to Montgomery, he was exhausted. In October, the city authorities tried to outlaw MIA's car pool by declaring it a "public nuisance." King feared he would have no choice but to end the boycott. But on November 13, 1956, the U.S. Supreme Court announced its ruling,

firmly declaring Alabama's bus segregation laws to be unconstitutional.

On December 20, 1956—381 days after the bus boycott had begun—the historic court ruling became law in Montgomery. The following morning, King and his associates delightedly took the first unsegregated ride around the city. Despite some severe outbreaks of violence—Ralph Abernathy's house and church were bombed in January 1957, for example—the sight of blacks and whites riding the buses together soon became commonplace. The "miracle of Montgomery" had come to pass.

Following the bus boycott victory, King legally was able to take his seat next to Glenn Smiley, a minister and supporter who taught him how to use nonviolent tactics.

CHAPTER FOUR

CONTINUING THE STRUGGLE

Events in Montgomery had brought King nationwide fame, as well as the respect of thousands of Americans, both black and white. A humble man, King did not dwell on success. Instead, he turned his attention to the even greater struggle for equality that lay ahead.

THE 1957 CIVIL RIGHTS ACT

On May 17, 1957, King took part in a prayer pilgrimage to Washington, D.C., where he addressed his fellow black pilgrims on the subject of voting rights. The Fifteenth Amendment to the Constitution had given all black men the right to vote. This was later extended to women. By a variety of means, however, including the introduction of literacy tests that many blacks did not have the education to pass and poll taxes they did not

have the money to pay, many state governments had effectively denied this right. Now, King declared, was the time to claim it back.

Dwight D. Eisenhower, the U.S. president who took office in 1952, had not been a great champion of the black cause, but his administration had put a piece of civil rights legislation before Congress. Following opposition from southern members, a diluted version of this measure became law in August 1957. The 1957 Civil Rights Act committed the federal government to "securing and protecting" the black right to vote. It also established a Civil Rights Commission to investigate cases in which voter registration was blocked.

From the steps of the Lincoln Memorial, King addresses the crowd at the end of the Washington Prayer Pilgrimage.

CRISIS IN LITTLE ROCK

The urgent need to resolve the school segregation issue became abundantly clear in 1957. In the fall of that year, nine black students tried to enroll in Central High School, a segregated school in Little Rock, Arkansas. Although they had every right to do so, the state governor, Orval Faubus, called in the National Guard to prevent them from entering the school. A federal court quickly ordered Faubus to remove the guards, allowing the students to enter. A 500-strong white mob then went on the rampage outside the school.

Eventually, President Eisenhower had to send in U.S. Army troops to restore order and protect the nine students for the rest of the school year. By the fall of 1958, when enrollment was due to begin again, Faubus had shut down the school. It did not reopen until late in 1959. King hoped that the whole frightening—yet somehow ridiculous—episode would encourage nationwide debate of the school integration issue and put pressure on Southerners to change their racist ways.

THE SCLC

The act greatly disappointed King. The voting rights measure was vague and had no time limit, while a measure allowing the federal government to enforce schools desegregation had been totally removed. In August, therefore, he invited 115 black leaders to Montgomery to plan a civil rights strategy for the coming years. Together they set up the Southern Christian Leadership Conference (SCLC), with King as president. King's responsibilities increased still further in October when his second child, Martin Luther King III ("Marty"), was born.

A NEAR MISS

The pace did not slow in 1958. In the early months of the year, two particular enterprises occupied much of King's time. The first was a book about the bus boycott, which he completed with the help of Bayard Rustin, a member of CORE, in May. The second was the Crusade for Citizenship, an SCLC operation launched in February. The aim of this operation was to greatly increase the number of black people registered to vote in the South. Early results, however, were disappointing.

King's book was published in September 1958. Called *Stride Toward Freedom: The Montgomery Story*, it was highly praised by many reviewers. As part of a promotional tour, King visited New York. While he was in Blumstein's Department Store signing copies of the book, a black woman approached him and stabbed a letter opener into his chest.

In the uproar that followed, King had the sense not to remove the blade, which would have increased the bleeding. Instead he waited until an ambulance arrived to take him to Harlem Hospital. There, surgeons took out the weapon, later telling King that if it had been even a little closer to his aorta, he would have died. The police soon discovered that the would-be assassin, Izola Curry, was mentally ill. At King's insistence, she was sent to a hospital rather than a jail.

King with his mother (left) and wife in Harlem Hospital, after he was stabbed in a New York store.

During the last months of 1958, King had little choice but to rest. Then, in February 1959, he and Coretta visited India to see the places where Gandhi had once lived and worked. King was horrified by the squalor that he saw there, but he was also impressed by government efforts to improve the lives of the poor. Returning home, he recommitted

Martin Luther King Jr., his wife Coretta, and Indian Prime Minister Jawaharlal Nehru (center), in India in early 1959.

himself to his own struggle and to the non-violent principles he shared with Gandhi.

RETURN TO ATLANTA

King was soon back in the thick of the voting rights campaign, and he was now intent on broadening the SCLC's work. Progress towards the desegregation of schools and other public facilities remained slow and was likely to remain so unless pressure was applied to state governments and the federal government.

The SCLC was based in Atlanta, Georgia, while its president and guiding light—King himself—was a full-time minister in Montgomery, Alabama. King eventually decided he would have to return to Atlanta so that he could devote himself more fully to the civil rights cause. But he did not intend to give up the Christian ministry completely. Back in Atlanta, he would preach part-time at his father's Ebenezer Baptist Church. King and his family left Dexter Avenue in January 1960. It was a sorrowful parting but one which he knew was necessary.

STUDENTS AND SIT-INS

As the King family was settling into their new Atlanta home, another event in the civil rights struggle occurred. On February 1, 1960, four black students from the North Carolina Agricultural and Technical College sat down at a lunch counter in a Woolworth's store in the town of Greensboro. Because the counter was designated as for whites only, the students were ignored. Instead of leaving, however, they stayed and insisted on service.

There were sit-ins at the same Woolworth's counter for the rest of the week, the number of students involved growing daily. This simple yet effective tactic for opposing segregation was quickly and widely copied elsewhere. For example, about 500 students staged sit-ins at a variety of restaurants in Nashville, Tennessee, singing the protest anthem "We Shall Overcome."

The 1960 Woolworth's lunch counter sit-in. Other civil rights campaigners staged swimming pool "wade-ins" and church "pray-ins."

SNCC

King watched this new movement with approval. He was glad students had joined the struggle, and he was happy to give them advice when asked, always stressing the importance of nonviolence. In April 1960, King attended a student conference at Shaw University, in North Carolina. As well as giving the keynote speech, he urged participants to form an organization to coordinate student protests on different campuses.

Later that month, after discussing the idea, the students acted on King's advice and set up the Student Non-Violent Co-ordinating Committee (SNCC—pronounced "snick"). King had thought that it might become part of the SCLC, but, although the two groups shared many ideals, SNCC chose to be independent.

HARD LABOR

In October 1960, King became more directly involved in the student movement. Since the beginning of the fall term, young black men and women from Atlanta colleges had been staging antisegregation protests. Eventually, they persuaded King to join them at a sit-in. The location was Rich's, a snack bar in a city department store. Before long, the participants were arrested for trespassing and taken to jail.

At first it seemed all might be well. Atlanta's mayor promised to help desegregate eating places and released the students. King, however, was tried for a minor traffic offense he had committed in a neighboring county long before and sentenced to four months' hard labor. Worse still, he was sent to the notoriously harsh Reidsville Penitentiary. After just two days, however, King was mysteriously released.

The mystery of his release was soon solved. A presidential election was coming up in November 1960, and King had already met the Democratic Party candidate, Senator John F. Kennedy. It was this man, together with his brother and campaign manager Robert Kennedy, who had secured King's release. Kennedy went on to win the election, and King fervently hoped that the new president would prove a stronger advocate of civil rights than his fence-sitting predecessor.

KING AND KENNEDY

Kennedy was inaugurated in January 1961— the same month that King's third child, a boy named Dexter, was born. The new president did not immediately make plans for new civil rights legislation, fearing this would only stir up southern opposition in Congress. Instead, he used his executive powers to further the cause. In particular, he ordered the attorney general—his brother, Robert Kennedy—to extend both the voting rights and school desegregation campaigns in the South.

To demonstrate his personal commitment to equality, President Kennedy also appointed many black people to top government jobs. For example, Thurgood Marshall, the NAACP lawyer who argued the *Brown* v. *Board of Education* case, was made a judge in a New York Court of Appeals. King had hoped for more dramatic progress, however, and expressed his disappointment to President Kennedy when they met in the spring.

THE FREEDOM RIDES

Many civil rights organizations shared King's sense of disappointment. Among them was CORE, whose members decided to take action. Back in 1946, the Supreme Court had ruled that segregation on interstate trains and buses was illegal. Then, in the 1960 *Boynton* v. *Virginia* case, it banned segregation at

interstate bus and railway stations. Across the South, these rulings were being widely disregarded. CORE's aim was to bring this state of affairs to national attention.

CORE's chosen method was to set out on interstate trips they called "Freedom Rides," traveling from Washington, D.C., to New Orleans, Louisiana, on two buses. The passengers, who included both blacks and whites, were to travel and disembark together at terminals and see how local authorities reacted. The buses left the capital in May 1961. When they reached Anniston, Alabama, one vehicle was set on fire. Then, in Birmingham, Ku Klux Klan members attacked the Freedom Riders with baseball bats.

There was worse to come. The few riders who chose to continue made their way to Montgomery, where they were attacked by a 1,000-strong white mob. The police were reluctant to intervene and the segregationist Alabama state governor, John Patterson, refused to call out the National Guard. When King arrived to support the Freedom Riders, the situation grew yet more tense. Finally, President Kennedy sent in 600 federal marshals to protect the Freedom Riders and restore order.

Both John and Robert Kennedy were sympathetic to the black cause, but the President thought the Freedom Rides were unhelpfully inflammatory. He was also angry because they were distracting him from foreign policy clashes with the Soviet Union.

Throughout the summer Robert Kennedy struggled to stop further protests. In September, he finally persuaded the Interstate Commerce Commission to issue an order outlawing

In early 1961, J. Edgar Hoover, head of the FBI, began a surveillance operation on King.

When this "Freedom Ride" bus stopped outside Anniston, Alabama, in 1961, white racists firebombed it.

segregation on buses and in terminals once and for all. A short time afterward, the victorious campaigners ended their rides.

THE ALBANY MOVEMENT

Another campaign soon demanded King's attention. In December 1961, he was called to Albany, Georgia, where the struggle to desegregate public facilities was in full swing. The city leaders, backed by police chief Laurie Pritchett, were stubbornly resistant. King was reluctant to go, as SNCC, which often resented his involvement, was very active in the area. But Dr. William G. Anderson, leader of the Albany Movement, pleaded with him, and he decided to make the journey.

King and the SCLC organized a huge range of marches, sit-ins, and other antisegregation protests in Albany. Pritchett, however, was too wily to beat black protesters in full view of television cameras, knowing this would provoke federal intervention. Instead, he put them all in jail. King himself spent time in prison but was always released so that he

could not attract publicity. By August 1962, it was clear the campaign was failing, so it was ended. The poorly planned enterprise had achieved little apart from worsening tensions between the SCLC and SNCC, which was increasingly critical of King's tactics.

TROUBLE IN MISSISSIPPI

The civil rights struggle received another blow in September 1962, when black student James Meredith tried to enroll at the all-white University of Mississippi in Oxford. The Kennedys had sent federal marshals to protect him, but he was turned away by National Guard acting on the orders of state governor Ross Barnett. A second enrollment attempt led to a riot in which two people were killed. Meredith was eventually able to enroll on October 1 but only after the federal government had ordered in troops.

King was appalled by this episode and partly blamed Kennedy's lack of commitment to total desegregation. The incident also stiffened his resolve. The coming year, 1963, would mark the 100th anniversary of the Emancipation Proclamation. This year, he thought, was surely the time to settle the segregation issue once and for all.

CHAPTER FIVE

BIRMINGHAM AND AFTER

The Albany Movement's failure caused King much heartache, and he longed for another chance to prove that nonviolent protest could work. When, in 1963, the chance arose to launch a new campaign, he agreed. The site was to be Birmingham, Alabama, and King's main adversary the fearsome police commissioner Eugene "Bull" Connor.

A NEW APPROACH

King and his fellow SCLC members were invited to Birmingham by the Reverend Fred Shuttlesworth, head of the Alabama Christian Movement for Human Rights (ACMHR). Shuttlesworth had been trying to desegregate the city's public facilities but had made little progress against violent opposition.

The lessons of Albany had not been wasted on King. He knew now that careful planning and selection of targets were the keys to success. At a three-day meeting, he and the SCLC prepared their strategy in detail. First, they would stage a few shop sit-ins. Then they would hold street protest marches. King knew such tactics might provoke Connor to violence. He also knew that if pictures of this violence were broadcast on television, the federal government would have to act.

THE BATTLE OF BIRMINGHAM

Coretta gave birth to the Kings' fourth child, a girl named Bernice, who was known as Bunny, on March 28, 1963. Then, on April 3, the Birmingham campaign began with sit-ins at five department stores. At the same time, King issued the "Birmingham Manifesto," which demanded the desegregation of all store facilities, the hiring of black people by local businesses, and the formation of a bi-racial committee to draw up a timetable for total desegregation. Slowly, more and more blacks joined King's operation, learned non-

violent protest techniques, and marched through the streets.

"Bull" Connor's response to the protests was to throw hundreds of the participants into jail. After King took part in a march on April 13—Good Friday—he was himself imprisoned. While in solitary confinement, he read a statement about his campaign in a local newspaper. Written by eight white clergymen, it said King's protests were poorly timed and unnecessary. The statement also urged the black community not to get involved in direct action but to fight for their cause in the courts.

King responded to this statement with his famous "Letter from the Birmingham Jail." Writing mostly on scraps of paper, he outlined the reasons for the civil rights movement and defended his belief in nonviolent direct action. He also denied the clergymen's accusation that his movement was extremist and warned that violent separatist groups would grow if peaceful protest made no headway.

THE CHILDREN'S CRUSADE

By the time King was released from jail on April 20, the Birmingham campaign was fading. He and his SCLC staff decided to reinvigorate the protests by involving more black students. Younger children soon began asking to participate. At first, concerned these boys and girls might get hurt, King was reluctant to approve the plan. But then he realized their presence would capture the attention of the world like nothing else before.

The so-called Children's Crusade began on May 2 with a 1,000-strong march through Birmingham. As usual, Connor and his men waded in to arrest hundreds of participants. The next day, a 6,000-strong march took place, and the police chief responded more harshly. First, he ordered firemen to turn their

A police dog rips the clothing of a terrified marcher during the 1963 Birmingham Children's Crusade.

hoses on demonstrators, so that powerful jets of water knocked them to the ground. Next, he ordered the police to let their German Shepherd dogs loose on the terrified crowds.

REACHING AGREEMENT

As King had predicted, television viewers who saw these attacks were outraged. Leading politicians, including President Kennedy, rushed to express their horror and to condemn the Birmingham authorities. Meanwhile, King continued the marches, and Connor, failing to learn from his mistakes, continued his violent attempts to control them. Soon the city's jails were full to burst-

ing with school-age "criminals."

The federal government could not let the situation continue, so Attorney General Robert Kennedy and his staff set out to break the deadlock. Eventually, they were able to arrange negotiations between Assistant Attorney General Burke Marshall, King and his team, and local businesspeople. On May 10, an agreement was reached that met all three demands in King's manifesto. Although unrest continued for months, the city had taken a giant step away from its Jim Crow past.

KENNEDY AND CONGRESS

The events in Birmingham sparked other protests across the United States. They also prompted President Kennedy to take action. He prepared the way with a televised speech on June 11, 1963, in which he discussed how the civil rights issue should be tackled. In doing so, he made his own view clear. "The time has come," he said, "for America to remove the blight of racial discrimination and fulfill her brilliant promise."

Just eight days later, on June 19, Kennedy submitted a major new civil rights bill to Congress for approval. Among its most important proposals were measures to outlaw segregation in public places and to give the federal government power to enforce school desegregation. King was delighted but knew the bill would face opposition, especially from southern senators. He decided to keep up the pressure.

GROWING OPPOSITION

In the summer of 1963, black people waged nonviolent campaigns against discrimination in about 900 cities across the United States.

King disagreed with the violent approach of Malcolm X (below right) to the civil rights struggle but described him as a "sweet spirit."

Meanwhile, King toured the country giving speeches on the civil rights movement. In general, he was welcomed and applauded. Increasing numbers of blacks, however, including members of a militant group called the Black Muslims, were turning against his nonviolent approach.

King's most outspoken black opponent during this period was Malcolm X. A young, charismatic Black Muslim, he was regularly interviewed by journalists and always fiercely proclaimed that self-restraint would never produce equality for blacks. Instead, he said, blacks should not hesitate to use violence against whites and should also establish a separate black state. Malcolm X denounced Martin Luther King as "a little black mouse sitting on top of a big white elephant."

THE MARCH ON WASHINGTON

Despite these challenges, King forged ahead with the campaign to pressure Congress. The centerpiece was to be a huge march in Washington, D.C., organized by King and other prominent black activists. Many people were against the demonstration, fearing it would only stir up opposition, but King was determined it should take place.

The date set for the March on Washington was August 28. King was one of many civil rights leaders scheduled to speak when the marchers reached the Lincoln Memorial. The night before, he worked for hours on the speech, knowing it would be a unique opportunity to address thousands of people directly, as well as to be heard by television viewers around the globe. It was to be the most memorable speech of his career.

The march was a great success. About 250,000 people peacefully made their way to the Lincoln Memorial, where they joined in prayers and listened to many speeches, spirituals, and gospel songs. King's speech was the last of the day. Toward the end, he spoke spontaneously and poignantly about his dream for the future of the United States:

> " I have a dream that one day ... the sons of former slaves and the sons of former slaveowners will be able to sit down together at the table of brotherhood.... I have a dream that my four little children will one day live in a nation where they will not be judged by the color of their skin but by the content of their character. I have a dream today. "

DEATH OF A PRESIDENT

The March on Washington provided a boost to King and the civil rights movement but was not able to wipe out opposition to Kennedy's proposed new legislation. On the contrary, a southern filibuster in the Senate blocked its path into law. While the political

King's historic "I Have A Dream" speech was heard not only in Washington, D.C., but also by millions of television viewers worldwide.

debates continued, tension flared in the South. On September 15, a bomb exploded at the Sixteenth Street Baptist Church in Birmingham, killing four black girls.

On November 22, another untimely death occurred. As his motorcade was making its way through Dallas, Texas, President Kennedy was shot in the head. He died less than an hour later. Lyndon B. Johnson, Kennedy's vice president, was quickly sworn in as the new U.S. president. Soon afterward, Johnson pledged support for the stalled civil rights bill. King was greatly relieved.

THE 1964 CIVIL RIGHTS ACT

True to his word, President Johnson used his considerable political skills to persuade southern Democrats to end the filibuster. On July 2, 1964, with King in attendance, he was finally able to sign the Civil Rights Act into law. Its main provisions were to make segre-

Lyndon B. Johnson is sworn in as the 36th president of the United States. Jacqueline Kennedy, the widow of his assassinated predecessor, stands by his side.

King holds pictures of James Chaney, Andrew Goodman, and Michael Schwerner, who were some of the civil rights workers murdered during the Freedom Summer.

gation in public places illegal and to establish the Equal Employment Opportunity Commission (EEOC), an agency with a mandate to fight racial discrimination in the workplace.

President Johnson and many other politicians believed that the passage of the new act would—and should—put an end to black campaigns for equality. King quickly pointed out that they were wrong. Among the difficulties still to be overcome, he asserted, was the denial of voting rights to thousands of blacks. As usual, he did not simply identify the problem but set out to find a solution.

THE FREEDOM SUMMER

Nowhere was it more difficult for blacks to vote than in Mississippi. There, blacks were routinely intimidated by whites as they tried to register. Ku Klux Klan violence was also widespread. In mid-1964, SNCC and CORE began a voter registration campaign in the state. King and his SCLC colleagues also toured the area, speaking in their support.

This so-called Freedom Summer bore bitter fruit. Six civil rights workers were murdered and more than 80 injured, while fewer than 2,000 new voters were registered. Faced with

this brutal reality, the campaign participants—many of them young idealists from the North—again began to question the value of King's nonviolent tactics.

PROJECT ALABAMA

Late in 1964, King learned he had won the Nobel Prize for Peace. He received the award in Norway on December 10 and then got back to business by preparing a new voting rights campaign. It was called Project Alabama, and its location was to be the city of Selma in that state.

The campaign began in January 1965. As tension grew, the SCLC organized a protest march from Selma to Montgomery, the state capital. It began on Sunday, March 7, while King was in Atlanta. After participants had walked a short way, state troopers attacked them with clubs and fired tear gas in their faces. Then, local sheriff Jim Clark and his men beat them with whips. The whole, shockingly violent episode, which became known as "Bloody Sunday," was televised nationwide.

King was horrified, and in response he arranged another march, this time of clergy from across the United States. It took place on March 9 but ended prematurely on King's orders. SNCC criticized this decision, believing King had caved in to an assumed threat from state police. Meanwhile, in Washington, President Johnson had already decided to act.

THE 1965 VOTING RIGHTS ACT

On March 15, in a speech to Congress, Johnson declared it was "deadly wrong" to deny any Americans the right to vote. He put forward a bill proposing a radical new voting rights act. As usual, King kept up the pressure. Beginning on March 21, he finally led a march the full 50 miles (80 kilometers) from Selma to Montgomery. At its end, on March 25, he made a speech in the city where he had begun his campaigning ten years before. The watching crowd of 25,000 joyfully sang "We *Have* Overcome."

The 1965 Voting Rights Act became law on August 6, 1965. The act banned literacy tests and all other restrictive practices in states where less than half the population had voted or registered to vote in 1964. It also

At a ceremony in Oslo, Norway, King receives the Nobel Prize for Peace from Gunnar Jahn, president of the Nobel Prize Committee.

arranged for the appointment of federal registrars, whose role was to visit southern states and ensure that black people could claim their right to vote without intimidation. A major victory had been won.

SHOWDOWN IN ST. AUGUSTINE

In spring 1964, before the passage of the Civil Rights Act, King received a call for help from the black community of St. Augustine, Florida. This town was the oldest permanent European settlement in the United States, and its white population was resisting all efforts to end segregation. King decided it would be an ideal location for further demonstrations, so he sent SCLC members to plan a campaign.

After organized action began in May, the local Ku Klux Klan responded with protests (right) and brutality. When King arrived, he asked the President to send in federal marshals to restore order, but Johnson refused. The trouble continued until June—during which King was briefly imprisoned for

requesting service in a whites-only restaurant—before Governor Farris Bryant set up a committee to work out a solution to the town's race problems. No changes were promised, but King could rightly claim that at least some progress had been made.

CHAPTER SIX

WHERE DO WE GO FROM HERE?

Once both the Civil Rights Act and the Voting Rights Act had become law, King pondered what to do next. He began to consider an issue that had been troubling him for some time—the situation of blacks in the North. They had not suffered official segregation like those in the South, but many thousands still lived in poor ghettos and had neither jobs nor hope for the future. King decided to turn his attention to their plight.

TAKING ACTION

There had been race riots in the cities of the North since the early twentieth century. Several had erupted during the summer of 1964, including one in New York. It was a riot in August 1965 that finally spurred King into action. The location was Watts, a black suburb of Los Angeles, and the spark was a policeman's attack on a member of a crowd protesting another man's arrest. Within six days, thirty-four people had been killed.

King made a brief trip to Watts. His northern campaign, however, would begin in Chicago. Having visited this city in July, he had seen the injustice and the school and housing segregation its black population faced. Local black activist Reverend Jesse Jackson was already leading an effective campaign there called "Operation Breadbasket." This campaign used boycotts and other tactics to persuade white owners of food shops and other businesses to hire black staff. The city was, therefore, an ideal site for a landmark struggle against discrimination.

KING AND VIETNAM

During this period, King had another major issue on his mind. The United States had been supporting noncommunist South Vietnam against communist North Vietnam since the 1950s. In 1965, President Johnson had begun to increase the country's military involve-

Firefighters in the Watts suburb of Los Angeles extinguished blazes in shops and other buildings during the 1965 race riot.

ment in Vietnam greatly, sending in 50,000 extra troops and promising more.

King was dismayed by this development, not only because he believed in nonviolence, but also because he thought the United States should not interfere in other countries. His criticism of American intervention brought condemnation, however, from the President and some of King's own SCLC allies.

THE CHICAGO CAMPAIGN

King's Chicago campaign began in January 1966. His first aim was to end the terrible conditions in the city's slums. Knowing this would involve taking on Richard J. Daley, the powerful mayor of Chicago, he moved into a rat-infested slum in the city in order to be close to the action.

Mayor Daley frustrated King's efforts without resorting to abuse or violence. For example, as soon as King began to criticize housing conditions, Daley started taking slum landlords to court, forcing them to repair their tenements. He publicized the city's slum improvement work in order to reduce complaints, with the clear message that King's intervention was unnecessary. Many Chicago residents, both black and white, agreed.

BLACK POWER

As the Chicago campaign stumbled on, there was a disturbing development in the South. In June 1966, James Meredith staged a one-man "March Against Fear" from Memphis, Tennessee, to Jackson, Mississippi. His goal was to show that blacks could now walk long distances without fear of attack and so should not be afraid to take short walks to polling places. In Mississippi, however, Meredith was shot by a white sniper.

Hearing this news, King flew to Memphis, where Meredith was in the hospital. Also at Meredith's bedside were Stokely Carmichael, leader of SNCC, and Floyd McKissick, head of CORE. The three leaders decided to organize a joint march from where Meredith was shot to Jackson. During the trek, they argued over nonviolence and white participation in the civil rights movement. King supported both, Carmichael and McKissick neither.

The conflict between the leaders came to a head when Carmichael declared to a crowd in Greenwood, Mississippi, that nothing had been achieved in six years of pleading for freedom and that a new slogan was needed: "Black Power." This slogan appalled King because it seemed to hint at the use of violence and black sepa-

ratism. Carmichael eventually agreed not to use the slogan until the march ended in Jackson. After the march, "Black Power!" became a rallying cry for many angry blacks across the nation.

CONFRONTATION IN CHICAGO

King made his way back to Chicago, where his family was spending the summer, and he began organizing a march on City Hall, the mayor's headquarters. The march took place on July 10, and more than 30,000 people participated. Once they reached their destination, King taped a list of demands to the door. Mayor Daley, however, was not at all impressed. The next day he told King in no uncertain terms to back off.

It was a blisteringly hot summer, and life in their dingy, cramped apartment was not pleasant for the King family. On the streets of the city, tensions had risen. Many young blacks rioted night after night. Working with Mayor Daley, King managed to restore some calm, then stepped up his nonviolent protest campaign. The plan was to march through neighborhoods where no blacks were able to live because residents and real estate agents worked together to keep them out.

The marches against segregated housing stirred up some of the most vicious opposition King had ever seen. But as whites hurled rocks, the protesters remained nonviolent. Eventually, Mayor Daley called King in for a meeting on August 26, and they worked out an agreement that committed the city to a more just housing policy. At first, King believed he had won. In fact, however, the agreement contained neither guarantees nor a timetable for change, and it had little long-term effect.

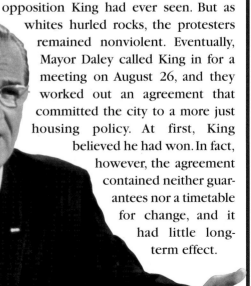

In his 1964 State of the Union speech, President Johnson committed himself to the fight against poverty in the United States.

WHERE DO WE GO FROM HERE?

King returned to Atlanta in the fall of 1966. There, he spent long hours brooding about the split within the civil rights movement between those who opposed and those who supported the use of violence. He was also depressed about the growing "white backlash" against black gains.

King discussed these issues and more in a book he wrote early in 1967. *Where Do We Go From Here?* outlined his opposition to what he saw as the destructive aspects of the "Black Power" movement. At the same time, it encouraged black people to continue the fight for equal treatment. King also developed a new strand of his thinking in this book. The struggle for justice, he said, should be widened to include other disadvantaged groups, from poor whites to Puerto Ricans.

(From left to right) King, the wounded James Meredith, Stokely Carmichael, and Floyd McKissick on the 1966 march to Jackson, MS.

OPPOSING VIETNAM

Developments in the Vietnam War also greatly troubled King at this time. Since President Johnson's original intervention, the number of American troops in the country had risen steadily, reaching almost 500,000 in 1967. These forces had fought many battles, with high death tolls on both sides, yet still victory was not in sight.

In King's view, the war was not only evil in itself, it was costing billions of dollars that could be better spent helping the poor at home. In addition, it was sending thousands of Americans—a disproportionate number of them black—to their deaths. Feeling morally obliged to take a stand, King made numerous antiwar speeches. On April 4, at the Riverside Church in New York, he even compared some American actions in Vietnam to actions of the Nazis and called for an immediate ceasefire.

The response was fierce. Many politicians and journalists criticized King for venturing

THE BLACK PANTHERS

The Black Muslims and SNCC were not the only organizations who denounced King's nonviolence. Equally, if not more, critical of his stance was the Black Panther party, a militant group founded by students Huey Newton and Bobby Seale in Oakland, California, in 1966. Its members wore military-style uniforms and were sometimes armed. They raised their right fists as a sign of their commitment to "Black Power."

into areas that were supposedly beyond his competence. Others called him as a closet Communist who wanted the North Vietnamese to win. King also faced opposition from the NAACP and other black leaders, who believed that by antagonizing President Johnson he was putting the civil rights cause at risk. Stokely Carmichael and SNCC, however, were glad to support him.

King was taken aback by the extent of the criticism. Nevertheless, he remained sure that he was right and agreed to participate in a major antiwar march in New York on April 15. Walking alongside 125,000 other protesters, including Carmichael, he made his way from Central Park to the United Nations building, then addressed the crowd. Always a patriot, King carefully distanced himself from demonstrators who burned an American flag and their draft cards.

THE POOR PEOPLE'S CAMPAIGN

During the summer of 1967, King watched in horror as race riots erupted in many northern cities. The worst riot was in Detroit, Michigan, where 43 people were killed in July. King's appeal to President Johnson to reduce the unemployment and poor housing conditions that fueled such outbursts proved fruitless, so he turned again to direct action.

As he had suggested in *Where Do We Go From Here?*, he intended to draw together people from many sections of society in a Poor People's Campaign. They would march from all across the United States to Washington, D.C., and then begin huge, lasting protests, during which protesters would camp in city parks. At the same time, King would demand that the government introduce a Bill of Rights for the Disadvantaged.

Even before King officially launched the Poor People's Campaign in December 1967, many people had voiced opposition. They included some black leaders who feared the demonstrations would descend into violence. President Johnson, who believed he had already done enough for poor blacks, considered the campaign a personal insult. He was also afraid it might bring chaos to the U.S. capital.

Despite all the criticism, King went ahead. His plan was that protesters should reach Washington in spring 1968, so he spent the New Year frantically making preparations. The pressure took its toll, leaving him tired and depressed. His anxiety was not only about the future of the movement, but also about his own fate. He had been receiving assassination threats for years, but they had begun to weigh on his mind as never before.

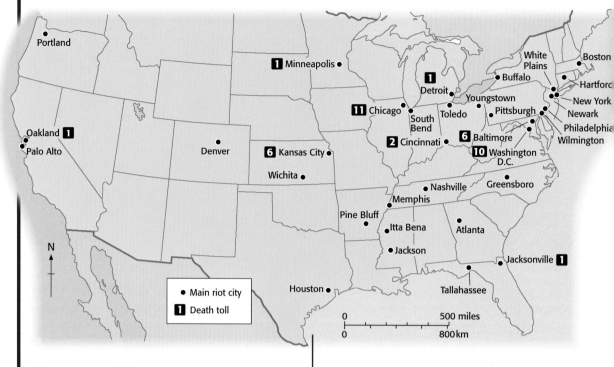

MAYHEM IN MEMPHIS

In February 1968, 1,300 garbage collectors from Memphis, Tennessee, went on strike because the city government had refused to increase their pay, improve their working conditions, or recognize their union. As 90 percent of the workers were black, they appealed to James Lawson, a member of the SCLC and pastor of the Centenary Methodist Church, for help.

Lawson asked King for support. King agreed, first addressing a rally in Memphis on March 18 and then returning to lead a protest march ten days later. As the march began, King positioned himself at the head of the crowd and started walking into the city center. During the march, members of a local black group called the Invaders began breaking shop windows and looting the stores. As soon as he became aware of the violence, King stopped the march.

It was too late, however, to prevent a riot. By the end of the rioting, a black boy was dead and 80 other people were wounded. The whole episode aroused more hostility

This map shows the main U.S. cities in which riots broke out after King's assassination in 1968. A total of 168 cities were affected.

against King. If he could not control these protesters, people asked, how could he claim there would be no violence in Washington?

A TRAGIC END

Thinking the matter over back in Atlanta, King decided that the only way to demonstrate his commitment to nonviolence was to return to Memphis once more. He called another march for April 5.

King arrived back in the city on April 3 with his trusted colleague Ralph Abernathy by his side. After checking in to the Lorraine Motel, the two men busied themselves with preparations for the march. In the evening, King delivered a heart-stopping speech at the Mason Temple. Reviewing his life, he thanked God he had not died when he was stabbed in 1958. Then he went on:

King on the balcony of the Lorraine Motel in Memphis where he was shot. To his left is Jesse Jackson and to his right Ralph Abernathy.

A veiled and grief-stricken Coretta King at her husband's funeral. Since his death, she has worked to preserve his memory.

> *We've got some difficult days ahead. But it really doesn't matter with me now. Because I've been to the mountaintop....And I've looked over. And I've seen the Promised Land. And I may not get there with you. But I want you to know tonight that we as a people will get to the Promised Land.*

The next day—Thursday, April 4, 1968—King and his team were due to have dinner at the house of local black pastor Samuel Kyles. Kyles came to pick them up some time after 5:30 P.M., but as they were about to leave, Abernathy asked King to wait while he put on some aftershave lotion. King then stepped out onto the balcony of his motel room and chatted with his other friends, who were already in the parking lot below.

The next second, a shot rang out, hitting King on the right side of the face and doing

terrible damage. Abernathy immediately came to his aid and an ambulance was called, but King was mortally wounded. He died at St. Joseph's Hospital at just after 7:00 P.M. He was buried in Atlanta on April 8. More than 50,000 mourners—including his beloved wife and children—attended his funeral. James Earl Ray, a white man who had been in and out of prison all his life, was convicted of the murder of Martin Luther King Jr.

PREACHER OR POLITICIAN?

Martin Luther King Jr. began his working life as a Baptist pastor and continued to preach throughout his career. Nevertheless, in 1960, he abandoned full-time ministry to devote himself to the struggle for black civil rights. In this role, for which he is chiefly remembered, King developed impressive political skills. In the courts and on the streets, quoting the Constitution as well as the Bible, he took on the American establishment and won major victories. Was King a political preacher, a religious politician, or a mixture of the two? Read both sides of the argument and the sources below, then judge for yourself.

PREACHER?

SOURCE 1

This is my being and my heritage for I am also the son of a Baptist preacher, the grandson of a Baptist preacher and the great-grandson of a Baptist preacher.
(MARTIN LUTHER KING JR.)

SOURCE 2

I came to see that God had placed a responsibility on my shoulders and the more I tried to escape it, the more frustrated I would become.
(MARTIN LUTHER KING JR.)

SOURCE 3

The teachings of the Great Three – Jesus, Thoreau, and Gandhi – have been brought together. . . . The new synthesis is known simply as a 'philosophy of love' . . . an alternative to the conflict and killing that we usually associate with social progress.
(EXTRACT FROM *CRUSADER WITHOUT VIOLENCE*, BY L.D. REDDICK)

A PREACHING TRADITION

Martin Luther King Jr. was born into a long line of Baptist preachers (*Source 1*). He grew up strongly aware of this rich tradition, which was reinforced every time he heard his father address the congregation at Atlanta's Ebenezer Baptist Church. King learned early that the preaching vocation did not mean that one need concern oneself only with the afterlife. His father worked tirelessly to help people on Earth.

King preaching at Ebenezer Baptist Church, in Atlanta.

FROM DOUBT TO FAITH

In his early teenage years, King rebelled against his father's clear expectation that he, too, would be a preacher. Not only did he doubt the truth of Christianity, but he also began to think there were better ways to serve the black community. At Morehouse College, however, he learned about a more liberal form of Christianity that he could accept. By the age of 17, King was committed to becoming a minister (*Source 2*).

A NEW PHILOSOPHY

After King was ordained in 1948, he divided his time between continuing his education and preaching. While at both Crozer and Boston University, he read widely. He read from the Bible,

of course, but also from the works of Gandhi and many others. By 1954, when he began his ministry at Dexter Baptist Church in Montgomery, King had devised a philosophy that combined many ideals (*Source 3*). At its heart was a deeply Christian notion that ordinary believers might have to suffer as Jesus had suffered in order to change the world for the better.

MONTGOMERY AND AFTER

During his five-and-a-half years in Montgomery, King earned a reputation as a skillful preacher whose oratory could inspire both the illiterate and the educated. His fame was such that he was invited to give sermons in many other churches. It was also during this period that he first experienced the sense that God was speaking through him in his sermons. Even after 1960, when King left Montgomery to work for the SCLC in Atlanta, he did not give up preaching. On the contrary, he again became copastor at his father's church.

PREACHING WITHOUT A PULPIT

Once he began his civil rights work in earnest, King used his preaching gift to influence a far wider audience. Whether at small meetings or major rallies such as the 1963 march on Washington, he employed ringing phrases, heartfelt pleas, and mesmerizing repetition to drive his message home. Often black audiences would respond as though in church (*Source 4*). King's "political" speeches, thus, were really a form of preaching without a pulpit (*Source 5*).

A PREACHER AT HEART

Although King spent most of his adult life struggling to win political and economic rights for the black people of the United States, he did so as a preacher, not a politician (*Source 6*). He was never interested in gaining power for himself. Instead, he was interested in using his talents—and, if necessary, suffering—to convey his faith and turn his dreams of a better future into reality.

King at a service for James Reeb, a pastor killed at Selma.

SOURCE 4

I come to tell you tonight in Selma, you may not have a lot of money (No), you may not have degrees surrounding your name . . .; you may not know all the intricacies of the English language (No); you may not have your grammar right (Right); but I want you to know that you are as good as any Ph.D in English (shouts and applause). I come to Selma to say to you tonight that, oh, (Speak! speak!) that you are God's children and therefore you are somebody (tumult).
(KING SPEAKING IN SELMA IN 1965. THE WORDS IN BRACKETS ARE THE AUDIENCE RESPONSE.)

SOURCE 5

The substance of [his] sermons he translated into civil religious addresses and fiery mass-meeting speeches, but it was always preaching that he was doing. Even when no [Bible] text was cited and the deity [God] was not mentioned, the audiences to these speeches considered themselves no less a congregation.
(EXTRACT FROM *THE PREACHER KING: MARTIN LUTHER KING, JR. AND THE WORD THAT MOVED AMERICA*, BY RICHARD LISCHER)

SOURCE 6

In the quiet recesses of my heart, I am fundamentally a clergyman, a Baptist preacher.
(MARTIN LUTHER KING JR.)

PREACHER OR POLITICIAN?

POLITICIAN?

SOURCE 7

I have passed spots where Negroes had been savagely lynched . . . had seen police brutality with my own eyes and watched Negroes receive the most tragic injustices in the courts.
(EXTRACT FROM STRIDE TOWARD FREEDOM, BY MARTIN LUTHER KING JR.)

SOURCE 8

Unjust laws exist: shall we be content then to obey them, or shall we endeavour to amend them, and obey them until we have succeeded, or shall we transgress [break] them at once? Men generally . . . think that, if they should resist, the remedy would be worse than the evil. But why does it [the government] not encourage its citizens to be on the alert to point out its fault . . . ?
(EXTRACT FROM CIVIL DISOBEDIENCE (1849), BY HENRY DAVID THOREAU)

SOURCE 9

I was so deeply moved that I reread the [Thoreau's] work several times. This was my first intellectual contact with the theory of nonviolence and resistance.
(EXTRACT FROM STRIDE TOWARD FREEDOM, BY MARTIN LUTHER KING JR.)

WORKING FOR CHANGE

There is no doubt that in all he did, King was inspired by his Christian faith. He also had the training and instincts of a preacher. Nevertheless, once he left full-time ministry in 1960, he had to become a politician in order to succeed in his chosen task. This does not mean that he joined a party or stood for election. Rather, he engaged in politics in its broadest sense, understood as activities designed to produce social and economic change.

King at the White House in 1963, where he met President John F. Kennedy (fourth from the right).

EARLY INFLUENCES

From a young age, King was shocked both at the injustice black Americans suffered (*Source 7*) and at the government's failure to help them. His reading of Thoreau while at Morehouse College introduced him to the idea of resisting such institutionalized prejudice using nonviolent means (*Sources 8* and *9*). King's later discovery of Gandhi's works strengthened his new ideals. In them, he saw how a religious man could engage fully in a political struggle for the sake of his people.

THE MONTGOMERY MINISTRY

Until King became minister of Dexter Avenue Baptist Church in 1954, he had no opportunity to put his ideals into practice. Once there, he quickly set up a program to help the poor and became a member of the local NAACP committee. King's handling of the bus boycott and election as MIA president were clear early signs of his political skills. By the time he gave his speech at Holt Street Church, he was basing his arguments on political as well as religious texts (*Source 10*).

JUDGE
FOR YOURSELF

A NEW ROLE

After setting up the SCLC in 1957, King engaged in more political struggles that took him away from church work. By 1960, he could no longer combine the roles of preacher and politician, so he chose the latter (*Source 11*). Soon after he began working for the SCLC full time, SNCC sit-ins and CORE "Freedom Rides" took place. The government was forced to act when the opponents of these demonstrations resorted to violence. It was a lesson that King the politician quickly learned.

POLITICAL TALENTS

During the major campaigns that followed, King used his political talents to great effect. Not only did he mastermind demonstrations, he also dealt skillfully with the authorities at every level. In Birmingham, for example, King openly defied police chief Eugene "Bull" Connor, knowing he would respond with violence and so earn condemnation. When meeting Presidents Kennedy and Johnson, by contrast, King used reasoned argument to make his case. But he was never afraid to oppose presidential policy and spoke out in particular against Johnson's intervention in Vietnam.

Coretta King celebrates Martin Luther King day, a national holiday to mark King's political achievements.

PRACTICAL POLITICIAN

King was a deeply religious man. But it was his political skills and his willingness to engage in political struggle that distinguished him from other black religious leaders. Without these qualities, he would never have helped to win freedom for his people and a place in history for himself (*Source 12*).

SOURCE 10

If we are wrong, the Supreme Court of this nation is wrong. If we are wrong, the Constitution of the United States is wrong. If we are wrong, God Almighty is wrong. If we are wrong, Jesus of Nazareth is merely a Utopian dreamer who never came down to Earth.
(MARTIN LUTHER KING JR. IN HIS SPEECH ABOUT THE BUS BOYCOTT, DELIVERED AT MONTGOMERY'S HOLT STREET BAPTIST CHURCH, DECEMBER 5, 1955)

SOURCE 11

History was calling him home to Atlanta, obliging him to abandon his role as a preacher with a concern for civil rights and become a militant movement leader with a private and abiding religious faith.
(EXTRACT FROM LET THE TRUMPET SOUND, A BIOGRAPHY OF MARTIN LUTHER KING JR., BY STEPHEN B. OATES)

SOURCE 12

Martin Luther King, Jr., was the conscience of his generation. A Southerner, a black man, he gazed upon the great wall of segregation and saw that the power of love could bring it down.
(EXTRACT FROM THE CITATION ACCOMPANYING THE AWARD OF THE PRESIDENTIAL MEDAL OF FREEDOM TO KING ON JULY 4, 1977)

NONVIOLENCE—EFFECTIVE OR NAIVE?

Martin Luther King began to formulate his philosophy of nonviolence during his college years. Later, as a civil rights leader, he claimed that nonviolent protest was the only way to bring about reform that was both practical and moral. During the 1960s, however, SNCC and other more radical groups questioned King's methods. They maintained that violence was a legitimate response to the discrimination and cruelty encountered by blacks. Was nonviolence the most effective way to secure change, as King believed, or was it simply a naive policy of only limited usefulness? Read both sides of the argument and the sources below, then judge for yourself.

EFFECTIVE?

SOURCE 1

Love your enemies, do good to those who hate you, bless those who curse you, pray for those who ill-treat you. If someone strikes you on one cheek, turn to him the other also.
(JESUS CHRIST, AS QUOTED IN THE GOSPEL OF LUKE, CHAPTER 6, VERSES 27–29)

SOURCE 2

I found that the term "passive resistance" was too narrowly construed [understood], *that it was supposed to be a weapon of the weak, that it could be characterized by hatred, and that it could finally manifest itself as violence, I had to . . . explain the real nature of the movement. . . . Maganlal Gandhi coined the word "Sadagraha." . . . But in order to make it clearer I changed the word to "Satyagraha"* [Sadagraha means "firmness in a good cause," Satyagraha means "truth force"].
(EXTRACT FROM *AN AUTOBIOGRAPHY*, BY M.K. GANDHI)

A NEW APPROACH

As a teenager, King thought nonviolence was a weak creed that could not defeat evil. The teachings of Jesus (*Source 1*) and Thoreau helped to change his mind. It was through reading Gandhi's autobiography that King realized that passive resistance was a form of strength (*Source 2*) and a way of overcoming injustice (*Source 3*).

THE MONTGOMERY MIRACLE

King preached nonviolence throughout the 1955–1956 Montgomery bus boycott, explicitly ruling out use of the murderous tactics favored by the Ku Klux Klan (*Source 4*). The willingness of blacks to follow his lead and the success of the boycott proved that nonviolent methods could work. King argued this point firmly in his 1958 book *Stride Toward Freedom*.

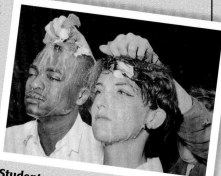

Students at a workshop learn how to remain nonviolent despite provocation.

PROVOCATION AND PUBLICITY

King's 1959 trip to India strengthened his commitment to Gandhi's way of nonviolence. Back home, he slowly increased his understanding of how best to follow it. The Freedom Rides taught him many lessons. He learned in particular that nonviolence could provoke violent reactions that brought to the

JUDGE
FOR YOURSELF

surface the brutality underpinning discrimination and that events like these could draw national publicity (*Source 5*).

ALBANY, BIRMINGHAM, AND SELMA
In the 1961–1962 Albany campaign, King hoped to put his new ideas into practice. However, the refusal of police chief Laurie Pritchett to use violence denied the protesters publicity and little was achieved. By contrast, during the 1963 Birmingham campaign, the brutal response of police commissioner Eugene "Bull" Connor brought TV coverage and the intervention of President Kennedy. In 1965, events followed a similar course in Selma, where "Bloody Sunday" caused President Johnson to act.

REASONS FOR RESTRAINT
During these campaigns, King often explained to protesters that nonviolent methods put them morally beyond reproach, making it hard for whites to justify violent responses. In addition, he noticed that whenever blacks had attempted violent revolts—for example, during slavery— white forces had crushed them. The same method, he declared, would still produce the same outcome.

The violent slave revolt led by Nat Turner in 1831 was quashed in just a few days.

KEEPING THE FAITH
When the Black Power movement emerged in 1966, King refused to abandon his principles. On the contrary, during the Chicago campaign he taught many more people the ideals and techniques of nonviolence. In 1967, King's book *Where Do We Go From Here?* and his anti-Vietnam speeches reaffirmed his opposition to all violence.

NECESSARY NONVIOLENCE
King believed nonviolence was effective, prevented an overwhelming white backlash, and was morally right. In his view, violence would lead only to the spiritual self-destruction of its perpetrators and a bitter, divided society (*Source 6*).

SOURCE 3
King thought Gandhi one of the great men of all time. "He was probably the first person in history to lift the love ethic of Jesus above mere interaction between individuals to a powerful effective social force on a large scale."
(EXTRACT FROM LET THE TRUMPET SOUND, A BIOGRAPHY OF MARTIN LUTHER KING, JR., BY STEPHEN B. OATES)

SOURCE 4
There will be no crosses burned at any bus stops in Montgomery. There will be no white persons pulled out of their homes and taken out on some distant road and murdered. . . . We are not . . . advocating violence. We have overcome that.
(EXTRACT FROM KING'S SPEECH AT HOLT STREET, DECEMBER 1955)

SOURCE 5
Without the presence of the press, there might have been untold massacre in the South. The world seldom believes the horror stories of history until they are documented via mass media.
(KING SPEAKING ABOUT THE FREEDOM RIDES)

SOURCE 6
I am convinced that if we succumb to the temptation to use violence in our struggle for freedom, unborn generations will be the recipients of a long and desolate night of bitterness, and our chief legacy to them will be a never-ending reign of chaos.
(MARTIN LUTHER KING JR.)

NONVIOLENCE—EFFECTIVE OR NAIVE?

NAIVE?

SOURCE 7

There are many of my poor black ignorant brothers . . . preaching the ignorant and lying stuff that you should love your enemy. What fool can love his enemy?
(ELIJAH MUHAMMAD)

SOURCE 8

I don't profess to have a political, economic, or social solution to a problem as complicated as the one which our people face in the States, but I am one of those who is willing to try any means necessary to bring an end to the injustices that our people suffer.
(MALCOLM X IN BY ANY MEANS NECESSARY: SPEECHES, INTERVIEWS, AND A LETTER, BY MALCOLM X)

SOURCE 9

Well I believe it's a crime for anyone who is being brutalized to continue to accept that brutality without doing something to defend himself. If that's how "Christian" philosophy is interpreted, if that's what Gandhian philosophy teaches, well, then, I will call them criminal philosophies. . . . I am for violence if non-violence means we continue postponing a solution to the American black man's problem.
(EXTRACT FROM THE AUTOBIOGRAPHY OF MALCOLM X)

ADVOCATES OF VIOLENCE

Some black Americans always opposed King's doctrine of nonviolence, believing it was a feeble response to injustice. It was not until the 1960s, however, that large numbers of blacks openly began to advocate violent tactics. For them, the Christian philosophy of loving resistance was not enough.

MALCOLM X AND THE BLACK MUSLIMS

In 1952, Malcolm X, a fiery young man who had led a wild life on the streets of Harlem, in New York City, joined an organization called the Nation of Islam. Its members, known as Black Muslims, believed that all black Americans were descendants of a Muslim tribe and should reject Christianity. The Nation's leader at the time, Elijah Muhammad, denounced nonviolence (*Source 7*) and urged black people to found a separate state within the United States.

Malcolm X soon became the Nation of Islam's spokesman, and in that role, he regularly clashed with King. They disagreed especially about the use of violence; Malcolm firmly maintained it could play a part in the black struggle (*Sources 8* and *9*). Although Malcolm X left the Nation of Islam in 1964, converted to orthodox Islam, and became less hostile to whites, he and his followers continued to believe that violence could be valid. Malcolm was shot dead by a Nation of Islam member in 1965.

Malcolm X speaking in Washington, D.C., in May 1963.

SNCC

Less militant organizations also turned against King's methods. Among them was the Student Non-Violent Co-ordinating

Committee. Its members were originally dedicated to non-violence, but white brutality changed their views. The terrible events of the 1964 Freedom Summer in Mississippi were a major turning point, but it was not until 1966 that SNCC commitment to non-violence finally dissolved.

BLACK POWER

Even after the Civil Rights Act and the Voting Rights Act, SNCC members felt little had changed. The "Black Power" slogan their leader Stokely Carmichael coined during the 1966 March Against Fear (*Source 10*) gave them a way to express their rage. When King took his nonviolent message to cities such as Chicago, SNCC and others responded with a new militancy (*Source 11*). Unsure about the value of King's tactics in the South, they considered them inadequate for riot-torn northern ghettos.

Militant H. Rap Brown urged blacks to move from "resistance to aggression."

FLAWED THEORY?

Not all opponents to King's nonviolence were against it because it had failed to produce the benefits they sought. Quoting black psychiatrist and social philosopher Frantz Fanon and others, some also claimed it was unhealthy for the oppressed not to strike back (*Sources 12* and *13*). Another criticism of King's approach was that it worked only when it provoked violence and, thus, was not really nonviolent at all.

NAIVE NONVIOLENCE

Opponents of King's nonviolent doctrine criticized it for a wide variety of reasons. Some thought it was ineffective and others that it was unhealthy. These critics agreed that it was a naive response to a serious and deeply rooted problem.

SOURCE 10

The only way we gonna stop them white men from whuppin' us is to take over. We been saying freedom for six years and we ain't got nothin'. What we gonna start saying now is Black Power!
(STOKELY CARMICHAEL, 1966)

SOURCE 11

Now it is over. The days of singing freedom songs and the days of combating bullets and billy clubs with love. . . . They used to sing "I Love Everybody" as they ducked bricks and bottles. Now they sing:
   Too much love,
   Too much love,
   Nothing kills a nigger like
   Too much love.
(SNCC MEMBER AND WRITER JULIUS LESTER. THE OFFENSIVE TERM "NIGGER" IS HIS.)

SOURCE 12

[Violence is] *a psychologically healthy and tactically sound method for the oppressed.*
(EXTRACT FROM *THE WRETCHED OF THE EARTH*, BY FRANTZ ANON)

SOURCE 13

By arguing that violence is as American as cherry pie . . . some have loudly advocated violence as the only appropriate means for achieving racial justice. To pretend otherwise would be equal to calling upon black men to contradict their own basic, natural, and . . . "healthy" tendencies.
(EXTRACT FROM *THE POLITICAL PHILOSOPHY OF MARTIN LUTHER KING JR.*, BY HANES WALTON JR.)

CIVIL RIGHTS LEGISLATION—SUCCESS OR FAILURE?

It was largely thanks to the efforts of Martin Luther King Jr. and his supporters that the 1964 Civil Rights Act and 1965 Voting Rights Act passed into law. At the time, these pieces of legislation were acclaimed as great milestones on the road to black equality. It soon became clear, however, that black Americans had many more obstacles to overcome. These obstacles included not only the difficulty of implementing the acts, but also problems that lay outside their scope, such as poverty. Was the civil rights legislation of the 1960s a success or a failure? Read both sides of the argument and the sources below, then judge for yourself.

SUCCESS?

SOURCE 1

Nobody needs to convince me any longer that we have to solve the problem [of racial injustice], not let it drift. . . .
(PRESIDENT JOHN F. KENNEDY, SPEAKING TO KING IN 1961)

SOURCE 2

REGISTRAR: What do you want?
CRAWFORD: I brought this lady down to register.
REGISTRAR: . . . Why did you bring this lady down here?
CRAWFORD: Because she wants to be a first class citizen like y'all.
REGISTRAR: Who are you to bring people down to register?
CRAWFORD: It's my job.
REGISTRAR: Suppose you get two bullets in your head right now?
(EXTRACT FROM A CONVERSATION BETWEEN SNCC MEMBER JAMES CRAWFORD AND A DEPUTY REGISTRAR IN LEE COUNTY, GEORGIA)

TWIN EVILS

Martin Luther King Jr. learned about the injustice of segregation as a child and continued to witness its damaging effects as he grew older. His concern with the deprivation of many of blacks' rights, including the right to vote, developed later but was no less strongly felt. King spent much of his life campaigning for federal legislation to outlaw these twin evils. His efforts were not in vain.

EARLY EFFORTS

President Eisenhower signs the 1957 Civil Rights Act.

Soon after King began his work, during the Eisenhower administration, the 1957 Civil Rights Act was passed. This measure failed to end the denial of black voting rights, even after it was strengthened in 1960. When John F. Kennedy was elected president, he vowed to support King's cause (*Source 1*), but he was reluctant to introduce new laws.

KENNEDY IN ACTION

Eager to change Kennedy's mind, King held many civil-rights campaigns in the early 1960s, such as the one in Albany, Georgia. Segregation and the obstacles put in the way of blacks who wanted to vote, however, persisted (*Source 2*). The violence that erupted during the 1963 protests in Birmingham finally spurred Kennedy into action (*Source 3*). He submitted a civil rights bill to Congress in June of the same year.

THE 1964 CIVIL RIGHTS ACT

The bill became law in July 1964, during the Johnson administration. This new Civil Rights Act included many measures for which King had struggled, such as an end to segregation (*Source 4*) and the establishment of an Equal Employment Opportunity Commission. It also gave the federal government extra powers to speed up school desegregation and to protect black voting rights. President Johnson believed that the Act would end racial discrimination in the United States.

CLAIMING THE VOTE

King realized the 1964 Civil Rights Act had given black Americans life-changing new freedoms. He also thought, however, it had deep flaws. The worst, in his view, was its failure to ban literacy tests and other tricks that whites used to stop blacks from voting. By early 1965, 3 million southern blacks were still not registered. The Selma campaign was designed to draw attention to this shameful fact (*Source 5*).

THE 1965 VOTING RIGHTS ACT

The violence in Selma led Johnson to prepare the Voting Rights Bill to guarantee blacks' right to vote. The bill became law in August 1965, and its effects were immediate. In state after state, blacks were able to register without intimidation, and numbers on the voting rolls rose sharply (*Source 6*). In 1952, only 20 percent of eligible southern blacks were registered. By the time of King's death in 1968, the figure was 60 percent.

SUCCESS STORY

The 1964 Civil Rights Act and the 1965 Voting Rights Act changed blacks' lives dramatically for the better. The former ended segregation, while also increasing educational and job opportunities. The latter allowed blacks to play their proper role in political life for the first time. Both were clear successes.

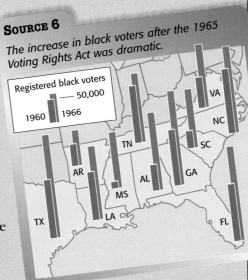

SOURCE 6

The increase in black voters after the 1965 Voting Rights Act was dramatic.

Registered black voters
— 50,000
1960   1966

VA
NC
TN   SC
AR   AL   GA
MS
TX   LA   FL

SOURCE 3

I shall ask the Congress . . . to make a commitment it has not fully made in this century to the proposition that race has no place in American life or law.
(EXTRACT FROM A TELEVISED ADDRESS MADE BY KENNEDY, JUNE 11, 1963)

SOURCE 4

SEC. 201 (a) All persons shall be entitled to the full and equal enjoyment of the goods, services, facilities, and privileges, advantages, and accommodations of any place of public accommodation, as defined in this section, without discrimination or segregation on the ground of race, color, religion, or national origin.
(EXTRACT FROM THE 1964 CIVIL RIGHTS ACT)

SOURCE 5

Why are we in jail? Have you ever been required to answer 100 questions on government, some abstruse [difficult to understand] even to a political scientist, merely to vote? Have you ever stood in line with over a hundred others and after waiting an entire day seen less than ten given the qualifying test? THIS IS SELMA, ALABAMA. THERE ARE MORE NEGROES IN JAIL WITH ME THAN THERE ARE ON THE VOTING ROLLS.
(EXTRACT FROM KING'S "LETTER FROM SELMA JAIL," WHICH HE WROTE IN 1965 WHILE IMPRISONED IN SELMA, ALABAMA)

CIVIL RIGHTS LEGISLATION—SUCCESS OR FAILURE?

FAILURE?

SOURCE 7

[I deplore the] *timidity of the federal government that is willing to spend millions of dollars a day to defend freedom in Vietnam but cannot protect the rights of its citizens at home.*
(KING SPEAKING IN SELMA, ALABAMA, IN 1965)

SOURCE 8

. . . even if we pass this bill, the battle will not be over. What happened in Selma is part of a far larger movement . . . the effort of American Negroes to secure for themselves the full blessings of American life.
(PRESIDENT JOHNSON SPEAKING ON MARCH 15, 1965, THE DAY HE SUBMITTED THE VOTING RIGHTS BILL TO CONGRESS)

SOURCE 9

Laws are passed in a crisis mood after a Birmingham or a Selma, but no substantial fervor survives the formal signing of legislation. The recording of the law in itself is treated as the reality of the reform.
(MARTIN LUTHER KING JR.)

SOURCE 10

UNITED STATES UNEMPLOYMENT
1963   4.8% white
        12.1% nonwhite

CHICAGO UNEMPLOYMENT
1966   2.3% overall
        13.0% black

THE BATTLE CONTINUES

The 1964 Civil Rights Act and 1965 Voting Rights Act were significant pieces of legislation. They were not, however, always put into practice effectively, and they failed to address many of the underlying problems faced by blacks in the United States. As a result, the black community had to continue its battles against discrimination long after the new laws were passed.

THEORY AND PRACTICE

The implementation of the 1964 Civil Rights Act was fraught with difficulty. Although it officially outlawed segregation, the unofficial separation of blacks and whites continued in many parts of the South, just as it did in the North. The law simply did not have the power to change the hearts and minds of whites who did not believe blacks were their equals.

Some have argued that there was also a gap between the theory and the practice of the 1965 Voting Rights Act.

Legislation did not address poverty in black ghettos.

Both before and after its introduction, King criticized the federal government's failure to protect Southern blacks who tried to vote (*Source 7*). The rise in the number of voters from August 1965 was by no means wholly due to government enforcement of the new law. Thousands of blacks were persuaded to register for the first time by student volunteers who toured the South. These same volunteers also pressured Congress to provide more registrars.

CONTINUING CONCERN

Both President Johnson and King openly acknowledged the limitations of the new legislation (*Sources 8* and *9*). The riots in Los Angeles and other cities shortly after the new laws were

A policeman frisks people in Detroit, Michigan, during a 1967 riot.

passed showed that their analysis was correct.

Over the following years, King repeatedly publicized the continuing problems of blacks, especially those in the northern ghettos. These problems included poverty, run-down, overpriced housing, and exclusion from better housing in white areas. Blacks also had to endure bad schools, inadequate health care, and high unemployment (*Source 10*). King urged both government officials and the public to assess the situation honestly, while Malcolm X cut to the heart of the matter with his usual candor (*Source 11*).

RIOT REPORT

From the mid-1960s, King campaigned for poor urban blacks, who the Civil Rights Act and the Voting Rights Act had hardly affected. "Black Power" advocates used their own techniques in pursuit of the same goals. Progress was slow and unrest continued; there were forty-three city riots in 1966 and eight more serious disturbances erupted in 1967. In response, Johnson ordered former Illinois governor Otto Kerner to chair an investigative commission. His 1968 report confirmed what King had long proclaimed (*Source 12*).

LIMITATIONS AND FAILURES

As King often pointed out, there are limits to what legislation can achieve. The Civil Rights Act and the Voting Rights Act outlawed many forms of racial discrim- ination, but they could not tackle deep-rooted social ills. In this sense, some believe they failed black Americans and left many feeling that the federal government did not care about their plight (*Source 13*).

Otto Kerner led the commission on the origins of race riots.

SOURCE 11

In this year, 1965, I am certain that more—and worse—riots are going to erupt, in yet more cities, in spite of the conscience-salving Civil Rights Bill. The reason is that the cause of these riots, the racist malignancy in America, has been too long unattended.
(EXTRACT FROM *THE AUTOBIOGRAPHY OF MALCOLM X*)

SOURCE 12

What white Americans have never fully understood —but what the Negro can never forget—is that white society is deeply implicated in the ghetto. White institutions created it, white institutions maintain it, and white society condones it. Our society is moving toward two societies, one black, one white—separate but unequal.
(EXTRACT FROM THE 1968 REPORT OF THE NATIONAL ADVISORY COMMISSION ON CIVIL DISORDERS, CHAIRED BY OTTO KERNER)

SOURCE 13

I feel that the federal government have proven that it don't care about poor people. Everything that we have asked for through these years had been handed down on paper. It's never been a reality. We the poor people of Mississippi is tired. We're tired of it so we're going to build for ourselves, because we don't have a government that represents us.
(THE WORDS OF MRS. UNITA BLACKWELL, A POOR BLACK WOMAN, IN 1966)

FIGHTING WAR AND POVERTY—RIGHT OR WRONG?

After the Civil and Voting Rights Acts became law, Martin Luther King Jr. still continued his campaigns on behalf of American blacks. At the same time, he began to address two other major issues—the growing involvement of the United States in the Vietnam War and the plight of all the poor in the country, from American Indians to Chicanos. In doing so, he earned more criticism than acclaim, especially from the Johnson administration. Was King right to condemn the Vietnam War and fight poverty, or was he wrong to meddle in matters outside the area of black civil rights? Read both sides of the argument and the sources below, then judge for yourself.

RIGHT?

SOURCE 1

When he accepted the Nobel peace prize he baptized all races into his congregation and confirmed the world as the battle-ground for his gospel of nonviolence and reconciliation. He is no longer—and probably never can be—a spokesman for just an American Negro minority.
(EXTRACT FROM AN ARTICLE BY FORMER SCLC MEMBER CHARLES FAGER IN THE *CHRISTIAN CENTURY* MAGAZINE)

SOURCE 2

We have destroyed [Vietnamese peasants'] most cherished institutions—the family and the village. We have destroyed their land and their crops. . . . We have corrupted their women and children and killed their men. What strange liberators we are!
(MARTIN LUTHER KING JR., SPEAKING ON APRIL 4, 1967)

ADDRESSING POVERTY

King began seriously to address the question of poverty in 1964. In his book *Why We Can't Wait*, he suggested creating a Bill of Rights for the Disadvantaged that would provide federal aid to all the poor people in the United States. In the same year, President Johnson committed himself to the fight against poverty by introducing a range of education and welfare programs that were intended to create a "Great Society" in which all Americans shared.

WORDS AGAINST WAR

For the next two years, King continued to devote himself mainly to the black cause, first in Selma, then in Chicago. At the same time, he began to speak out against Johnson's policy of increased intervention in the Vietnam War. King saw this stand as an inevitable consequence of his beliefs in Christianity and nonviolence. Many other people agreed (*Source 1*).

Robert Kennedy also spoke out against poverty and the Vietnam War.

WHERE DO WE GO FROM HERE?

In 1967, King began to address his two new themes —poverty across the racial divide and Vietnam—in earnest. The poverty issue

was much on his mind early in the year when he went to Jamaica to write a book. Called *Where Do We Go From Here?*, this book encouraged the poor of all races and creeds to unite in the struggle for justice. Back in the United States, King began to incorporate these ideas into his preaching.

ANTIWAR ACTIVITIES

Before King launched an all-out campaign against poverty, however, he turned his attention to Vietnam. Watching the horrors of the war on television convinced him he should be making greater efforts to end the fighting. Beginning in early 1967, he repeatedly denounced the conflict, most devastatingly in an address at Riverside Church, in New York, on April 4 (*Source 2*). These comments brought condemnation from politicians, conservative blacks in the SCLC and NAACP, and the press, but King had no doubt his actions were morally right (*Source 3*).

Facing opposition to his Vietnam policy, President Johnson did not run for reelection in 1968.

THE POOR PEOPLE'S CAMPAIGN

By the summer of 1967, it was clear that, despite the "Great Society" program, the American poor were still in dire need. Government money that might have helped them was being spent on Vietnam. King, therefore, decided to launch the Poor People's Campaign about which he had long dreamed (*Source 4*). His plan was that, in 1968, 3,000 people would march to Washington, D.C. Once there, they would hold mass demonstrations and demand the bill of rights King had proposed. Tragically, King did not live to see this dream fulfilled.

THE RIGHT WAY

King's activities after the Civil Rights Act and the Voting Rights Act became law were a continuation of his earlier work. He saw it as his Christian duty to fight for justice wherever the need arose, so it was right and logical for him to struggle against both war and poverty. As he stated in his "Drum Major Instinct" sermon, his aim was simply to serve (*Source 5*).

SOURCE 3

Now there are those who say, "You are a civil rights leader. What are you doing speaking out [against the Vietnam War]? You should stay in your field." Well, I wish you would go back and tell them for me that before I became a civil rights leader, I was a preacher of the Gospel. . . .
(MARTIN LUTHER KING JR., SPEAKING AT VICTORY BAPTIST CHURCH IN LOS ANGELES)

SOURCE 4

Gentlemen . . . we're going to reach out to the poor people in all directions in this country. . . . And we're going to bring them together and enlarge this campaign into something bigger than just a civil-rights movement for Negroes.
(MARTIN LUTHER KING JR., SPEAKING TO SCLC STAFF IN NOVEMBER 1967)

SOURCE 5

Every now and then I think about my own death, and I think about my own funeral. . . . I want you to say that day I tried to be right on the war question. . . . I want you to say that I tried to love and serve humanity. Yes, if you want to say that I was a drum major, say that I was a drum major for justice. Say that I was a drum major for peace. That I was a drum major for righteousness.
(MARTIN LUTHER KING JR., SPEAKING AT EBENEZER CHURCH, FEBRUARY 4, 1968)

FIGHTING WAR AND POVERTY—RIGHT OR WRONG?

WRONG?

If we are not with him [Johnson] on Vietnam, then he is not going to be with us on civil rights.
(WHITNEY YOUNG OF THE NATIONAL URBAN LEAGUE, SPEAKING TO KING)

SOURCE 7

Is he casting about for a role in Vietnam because the civil rights struggle is no longer adequate to his own estimate of his talents?
(EXTRACT FROM AN ARTICLE BY AMERICAN JOURNALIST MAX FREEDMAN)

SOURCE 8

At the end of October [1965] . . . the Bureau [FBI] requested another six-month authorization for wiretaps on SCLC's Atlanta headquarters. The intercepts, the Bureau told the Attorney General, had "provided considerable valuable intelligence information concerning communist influence on the SCLC through King, as well as the communist influence evident in the outspoken position which King has taken in opposition to the United States foreign policy concerning Vietnam."
(EXTRACT FROM *THE FBI AND MARTIN LUTHER KING, JR.*, BY DAVID J. GARROW)

MISGUIDED ACTIVITIES

By deciding to tackle war and poverty in the mid-1960s, King alienated large segments of American society. At the same time, his misguided new activities cast doubt on his own integrity, on his commitment to nonviolence, and on the validity of his previous civil rights achievements.

THE VIETNAM QUESTION

Nowhere was King more misguided than on the Vietnam question. Before he first spoke out, in 1965, SCLC advisers warned him it would be foolish to do so. In their view, criticism of American foreign policy would anger the president and reduce his support for the civil rights cause (*Source 6*). They feared that the public, then largely in favor of the war, might also react badly and decrease contributions to the SCLC.

Despite these warnings, King went ahead with his denunciations of the war. The results were even worse than predicted. Johnson and many members of Congress were furious, while some journalists wrote that vanity had deluded King into believing he could influence world politics (*Source 7*). J. Edgar Hoover and the FBI stepped up surveillance of King, falsely claiming he was influenced by Communists (*Source 8*).

BITTER BACKLASH

When King increased his antiwar comments in 1967, the backlash was even more bitter. After the Riverside Church speech, Johnson received a damning report about King from an advisor. Many newspapers were equally critical, claiming King did not know what he was talking about (*Source 9*). Even black leaders such as Roy Wilkins of the NAACP refused

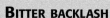
NAACP director Roy Wilkins disagreed with King's stance against the Vietnam War .

to back him. King's outspokenness made little difference to the war, but it did affect the civil rights movement. Once a supporter, President Johnson became distant, ignoring, for example, King's advice on the 1967 riots.

THE POOR PEOPLE'S CAMPAIGN

King's commitment to the Poor People's Campaign proved equally disastrous. When he first decided, in 1967, to go ahead with it, SCLC members warned him of the potential pitfalls—the huge cost, the difficulty of organizing such a vast operation (*Source 10*), and the possibility that it would unleash terrible violence that he could not control. President Johnson, meanwhile, expressed his outrage at the prospect, and the FBI, fearing a "true black revolution," began to watch King even more closely. He chose to ignore all these warning signs.

The Poor People's Campaign went ahead after King's death. A tent city was set up in Washington, but little was achieved.

King's participation in the Memphis garbage collectors' strike of 1968 was intended in part to be a miniature trial run for the Washington campaign. Sadly, it brought his movement into yet more disrepute (*Source 11*). His return to Memphis in April was designed to show that nonviolent protest could work, but the damage to the movement had already been done.

THE WRONG WAY

In concerning himself with war and poverty, King made a major error of judgment. Not only did he stray dangerously beyond his area of expertise, he also seriously damaged the civil rights movement and tarnished his own reputation. He had chosen the wrong way forward.

SOURCE 9

The Washington Post stated that King's criticism included "sheer inventions of unsupported fantasy."
... *By uttering "bitter and damaging allegations and inferences that he did not and could not document," the Post added, King "has done a grave injury to those who are his natural allies . . . and . . . an even greater injury to himself. Many who have listened to him with respect will never again accord him the same confidence. He has diminished his usefulness to his cause, to his country and to his people."*
(EXTRACT FROM *THE FBI AND MARTIN LUTHER KING, JR.*, BY DAVID J. GARROW)

SOURCE 10

You are attempting the impossible. There is no way for Martin Luther King to bring white poor, Puerto Rican poor, black poor, Irish poor together in any meaningful way.
(KING ADVISOR BAYARD RUSTIN)

SOURCE 11

Dr King's pose as a leader of a non-violent movement has been shattered. He now has the entire nation doubting his word when he insists that his April [Washington] project can be peaceful.
(EXTRACT FROM A MEMPHIS NEWSPAPER QUOTED IN *MARTIN LUTHER KING, JR. AND THE CIVIL RIGHTS MOVEMENT IN AMERICA*, BY JOHN WHITE)

FREE AT LAST—REALITY OR ILLUSION?

"Free at Last, Free At Last, Thank God Almighty, I'm Free At Last."
These words from a spiritual are carved on Martin Luther King Jr.'s tomb
in Atlanta's South View Cemetery. But did the civil rights movement that he
led so skillfully and at such personal cost really bring freedom to black
Americans? If so, have they been able to maintain and develop it in the
more than three decades since King's death? Read both sides of the
argument and the sources below, then judge for yourself.

REALITY?

SOURCE 1

*... the obligation of every
school district is to terminate
dual school systems at once.*
(EXTRACT FROM A RULING OF THE
U.S. SUPREME COURT, 1969)

SOURCE 2

U.S. BLACK PUPILS IN
ALL-BLACK SCHOOLS (%)

1968	64
1991	34

SOURCE 3

BLACK PEOPLE IN
WHITE-COLLAR JOBS (%)

1960	17
1976	33

SOURCE 4

*Among the EEOC's recent
litigation achievements are:
... over 5,000 entry level
and 34 management
trainee job offers to
qualified African American,
Hispanic, and female
applicants previously
denied positions.*
(EXTRACT FROM THE EQUAL
EMPLOYMENT OPPORTUNITY
COMMISSION WEB SITE)

A GREAT ACHIEVEMENT

It was Martin Luther King Jr.'s lasting achievement to establish
a legal framework that made freedom a possibility for all black
Americans. They have since continued the struggle to
make it an everyday reality.

DESEGREGATING SCHOOLS

A major advance
occurred just a year
after King's death. By
then, Richard Nixon was
president, and the 1964
Civil Rights Act was taking
effect. Some school
districts, however,
continued to block
desegregation, causing the
U.S. Supreme Court to rule that there should be no more
delays (*Source 1*). Because many schools were in all-white or
all-black areas, busing—that is, the transportation of pupils by
bus from one district to another—was introduced to help
ensure a racial mix in public schools (*Source 2*).

King's tomb in Atlanta, inscribed
with the words "Free At Last."

AFFIRMATIVE ACTION

In the 1960s, universities, businesses, and many other U.S.
institutions began affirmative action programs. The aim of
these programs was to help blacks and other minorities into
higher education and better jobs by encouraging them to
apply and by creating special programs for their admission.
Both the number of blacks in college and the percentage of
blacks in office jobs quickly rose (*Source 3*).

HIGH-PROFILE POSITIONS

Black Americans have also become far more visible in the national life of the United States, not only in the fields of music and sports, to which they have often felt confined by white expectations, but also in business and politics. After George W. Bush became president in 2000, he appointed two black people to his government team: Colin Powell, as secretary of state, and Condoleezza Rice, as national security advisor.

George W. Bush with Colin Powell (left).

THE EQUAL EMPLOYMENT OPPORTUNITY COMMISSION (EEOC)

The EEOC established by the 1964 Civil Rights Act still fights against discrimination on behalf of black people and other minorities (*Source 4*). On November 21, 1991, Congress also passed a new civil rights act that strengthened the legal provisions against racial discrimination in the workplace (*Source 5*). In February 1996, it introduced a new national enforcement plan to increase its effectiveness.

SIGNS AND SYMBOLS

Both federal and state governments have made important gestures acknowledging black contributions to American life and drawing a line under past discrimination. In 1983, for example, Congress made January 15—King's birthday—a national holiday. More recently, most states that have used the Confederate flag on their state flags have removed it or reduced its size, showing disapproval of racism (*Source 6*).

A poster in favor of Georgia's old flag, which was changed in 2001.

FREE AT LAST

Since the 1960s, black Americans have made great strides towards achieving the freedom that they have sought since the slavery era. They have not yet reached all their goals, but are free to do so, as the great progress they have made demonstrates.

SOURCE 5

*An Act
To amend the Civil Rights Act of 1964 to strengthen and improve Federal civil rights laws, to provide for damages in cases of intentional employment discrimination . . . and for other purposes. . . .*
(EXTRACT FROM THE CIVIL RIGHTS ACT OF 1991)

SOURCE 6

. . . I am . . . proud that we have come so far that my children find it hard to believe that we ever had segregated schools or separate water fountains labeled "white" and "colored." And I am proud that these changes came about because unity prevailed over division. Today, that same unity must be exercised again. The Confederate Battle Flag occupies two-thirds of our current state flag. Some argue that it is a symbol of segregation, defiance, and white supremacy, others that it is a testament to a brave and valiant people who were willing to die to defend their homes and health. I am not here to settle this argument . . . but I am here because it is time to end it. . . . Adopt [the new] flag and our people will be united as one rather than divided by race and hatred.
(GEORGIA GOVERNOR ROY BARNES SPEAKING ON JANUARY 25, 2001. THE STATE ADOPTED A NEW FLAG SIX DAYS LATER.)

JUDGE
FOR YOURSELF

FREE AT LAST—REALITY OR ILLUSION?

ILLUSION?

SOURCE 7

When Resurrection City closed down there was a sense of betrayal, a sense of abandonment. The dreamer [King] had been killed in Memphis and there was an attempt now to kill the dream itself.
(REVEREND JESSE JACKSON, SPEAKING ABOUT THE "TENT CITY" IN WASHINGTON)

SOURCE 8

. . . there goes all the progress, everything that's happened in the past ten years.
(OPINION OF A BLACK WORKER ON THE BAKKE RULING)

SOURCE 9

[t]he state shall not discriminate against or grant preferential treatment to, any individual or group on the basis of race, sex, color, ethnicity, or national origin in the operation of public employment, public education, or public contracting.
(EXTRACT FROM PROPOSITION 209)

SOURCE 10

UNEMPLOYMENT (%)

	Black	White
1980	14.5	6.1
1990	11.8	4.8
1994	13.9	6.7

(U.S. ECONOMICS AND STATISTICS ADMINISTRATION data)

FADING DREAMS

Black Americans' dreams of freedom began to fade immediately after King's 1968 assassination. Ralph Abernathy, King's successor, had neither his talents nor his charisma and was unable to bring the Poor People's Campaign to a successful conclusion (*Source 7*). The riots that took place after King's death also signaled a return to the past.

BUSING

Busing programs designed to integrate schools were often opposed by whites. Parents in Boston and Denver, for example, protested vigorously against local programs. As a result, Nixon tried to introduce an antibusing bill. In the *Milliken* v. *Bradley* case of 1974, the U.S. Supreme Court ruled that a Detroit busing program was unconstitutional because it stopped parents from having control over schools. Rich whites often simply avoided the issue by choosing private education for their children.

AFFIRMATIVE ACTION

Affirmative action programs have been similarly blocked. In a major legal case, white American Allan Bakke took the University of California to court. Bakke had failed to gain a place in its school of medicine in 1973. He later learned that black students with lower test scores had been admitted and that the "special admissions program" had only ever accepted blacks. On these grounds, Bakke claimed to be a victim of racial discrimination.

In 1995, the Nation of Islam organized the "Million-Man March" in Washington, D.C., to protest against continuing racism.

In 1978, the U.S. Supreme Court ruled in his favor. Many advocates of affirmative action were horrified (*Source 8*).

In 1997, the Supreme Court reached a decision on another major case. It allowed the addition to the California state constitution of Proposition 209, a law that banned affirmative action in the public domain (*Source 9*).

LIFE AND LAW

The fact that a few black Americans have made their mark in public life cannot disguise the truth that most blacks live far less well than their white counterparts. For example, compared to whites, black unemployment is higher (*Source 10*), black earning power lower (*Source 11*), and black life expectancy shorter (*Source 12*). In the ghettos, where drug addiction and violence are widespread, many young blacks now look to Malcolm X, not King, for inspiration (*Source 13*).

Rioting in Los Angeles following the 1992 verdict in the Rodney King case.

Discrimination against blacks by the police and in the legal system also remains a major problem (*Source 14*). One serious case in recent years was that of Rodney King, a black man beaten by Los Angeles police in 1991. A bystander videotaped the incident, and the tape was shown on television. When a jury found the police not guilty of brutality the following year, riots broke out, leading to the deaths of 53 people.

FAR FROM FREEDOM

King said that "Justice for black people will not flow into society merely from court decisions. . . . White America must recognize that justice for black people cannot be achieved without radical changes in the structure of our society." As many of those changes have yet to be made, justice—and the freedom that it makes possible—have yet to be achieved.

SOURCE 11

AVERAGE ANNUAL SALARY 1991

Black college graduates
$30,910

White college graduates
$37,490

(U.S. CENSUS BUREAU DATA)

SOURCE 12

MALE LIFE EXPECTANCY

	White	Black
1980	63	59
1985	74.6	65

(FIGURES TAKEN FROM *MAKING MALCOLM*, BY MICHAEL ERIC DYSON)

SOURCE 13

Everybody still listens to Malcolm X. When he talks you can't walk away. The thing about X is that he attracted and still attracts the people who have given up and lives recklessly – the crowd that just don't care what's going on. Making a difference in these people's lives is truly the essence of Malcolm X.

(RAPPERS ULTRAMAGNETIC MC's)

SOURCE 14

In Boston in April 1970, a policeman shot and killed an unarmed black man, a patient in a ward in the Boston City Hospital, firing five shots after the black man snapped a towel at him. The chief judge of the municipal court of Boston exonerated the policeman.

(CASE QUOTED IN *A PEOPLE'S HISTORY OF THE UNITED STATES*, BY HOWARD ZINN)

GLOSSARY

affirmative action: action designed to counteract discrimination against disadvantaged groups. Affirmative action programs often help black people get jobs or places in schools by making entry requirements more flexible for blacks and other minority groups.

attorney general: the chief law officer of the United States federal government and head of the Justice Department.

Black Muslims: a black religious movement established in the United States in 1930 and led from 1934 by Elijah Muhammad. Although Elijah Muhammad taught that black Americans were descended from a Muslim tribe, his teachings differed in many ways from orthodox Islam. More recently, the group has divided into two factions, one holding firm to Elijah Muhammad's teachings and the other embracing a more traditional form of Islam. The movement's alternative name is the Nation of Islam.

boycott: a protest that involves refusing to participate in an activity or buy a product. The aim of a boycott is usually to cause disruption or loss of earnings in order to persuade authorities to introduce change.

busing: the practice of transporting children by bus between schools in an effort to ensure racial integration in schools.

Chicano: a Mexican American.

civil rights: the personal rights of citizens that guarantee them certain freedoms, usually including freedom of speech and religion. In the United States, many civil rights are listed in the Bill of Rights, the first ten amendments to the Constitution that were adopted in 1791. King fought in particular to ensure that the rights guaranteed by the Thirteenth, Fourteenth, and Fifteenth Amendments were protected for black people.

colony: a territory ruled by another nation.

communist: a person who supports the political and economic system known as communism. Communism aims to create a classless society in which power and money are shared. Communist countries, such as the former Soviet Union and present-day China, are ruled by unelected members of a single political party. Under communism, businesses are owned and run by the state rather than by private individuals.

Confederacy: the 11 states of the southern United States that broke away from the country in 1860 and 1861, provoking the Civil War. The war ended in 1865, when Union forces defeated the Confederacy.

Congress: the law-making body of the United States, made up of the Senate and the House of Representatives.

Democratic Party: one of the two major political parties in the United States. The Democratic Party was founded in 1792, and many early presidents belonged to it. The party, however, was deeply divided over slavery. After the Civil War, it lost much of its influence to the Republican Party. During the 1930s and 1940s, under the leadership of President Franklin D. Roosevelt, the Democratic Party became more liberal. Presidents Kennedy and Johnson, both supporters of Martin Luther King Jr., were Democrats.

disenfranchisement: inability to vote, generally caused by either legal restrictions or intimidation.

divinity: *see* **theology**.

draft card: an official document issued by the United States government that requires a man to report for compulsory military service.

executive order: an order made by a U.S. president that does not have to be approved by Congress.

FBI (Federal Bureau of Investigation): an investigative agency that works to prevent spies and other enemies of the government from operating within the United States and also investigate violations of particular federal laws. The FBI is part of the Department of Justice.

federal marshal: a law enforcement agent whose main role is to protect the federal courts and to make sure that the U.S. judicial system works effectively. Some marshals also have wider law enforcement powers, including a duty to keep the peace.

filibuster: a deliberate attempt to prevent the passing of a bill through Congress by using delaying tactics such as extremely lengthy speeches.

grandfather clause: a law in some states of the southern United States that was designed to allow illiterate white people to vote while preventing black people from doing so. Grandfather clauses exempted people who had the right to vote on January 1, 1867, as well as their descendants, from electoral literacy tests. Since former slaves had not been granted the vote by that date, they had to take the tests—which were intentionally constructed to be extremely difficult—and so were still effectively disenfranchised.

Great Depression: the period of high unemployment and economic weakness that began with the 1929 collapse of the U.S. stock market. Much of Europe was also affected. The Depression eased by 1934 but did not fully end until the World War II era.

inaugurate: to install in office with a formal ceremony. United States presidents are normally elected in November and inaugurated in January of the following year.

Kingdom of God: according to Christian teaching, the reign of God on Earth, made possible through people's obedience to His will.

Nation of Islam: *see* **Black Muslims**

National Guard: the militias of the individual U.S. states. The National Guard is called on to maintain order during natural disasters and other disturbances. Its members serve as reserves for the U.S. armed forces.

Nazi: a member of the fascist National Socialist German Workers' Party, which ruled Germany during World War II under the leadership of Adolf Hitler. "Nazi" is a short form of the German words for "National Socialist."

pacifist: of or relating to the belief that violence of any kind, including war, is wrong.

penitentiary: a prison in which criminals are confined as punishment.

Ph.D.: the highest academic degree, which is awarded for original research. The abbreviation stands for Latin words meaning "Doctor of Philosophy."

poll tax: a tax collected from every adult, regardless of wealth, property owned, or income.

quota system: a system of allocating jobs, places in colleges, or similar competitive positions, in which a fixed proportion of jobs or places is allocated to a particular group.

Reconstruction: the period of United States history that immediately followed the Civil War and lasted from 1865 to 1877. During Reconstruction, the southern states rejoined the Union and rebuilt their war-torn territories. At first, the status of black people in the South also improved, thanks largely to pressure from the federal government. By the end of the era, when federal troops withdrew from the South, new institutions of racial discrimination were springing up.

Reformation: the religious movement that began in 16th-century Germany as an attempt to reform some practices of the Roman Catholic Church. The movement eventually became more wide-ranging and led to the establishment of Protestant churches. Martin Luther (1483-1546) was a major leader of the Reformation.

Republican Party: one of the two major political parties in the United States. The Republican Party was formed in 1854 and the first Republican president, Abraham Lincoln, was elected in 1860. Lincoln's anti-slavery stance precipitated the Civil War. Republicans remained dominant until Franklin D. Roosevelt was elected in 1932. Twenty years later, after World War II,

military hero and Republican Dwight D. Eisenhower was elected president, but he did little to further the civil rights cause.

secular: nonreligious.

seminary: an institution in which people train to become priests, ministers, or rabbis.

separatism: the view that different groups, such as racial, religious, or ethnic groups, should live in separate communities.

sharecropper: a farmer who works land rented from its owner in return for a share of the income from the crop produced. Many former slaves became sharecroppers on white-owned land after slavery was abolished. As sharecroppers, they remained largely under the control of whites.

state capitol: the building in which the law-making body of a U.S. state government meets.

Supreme Court: the highest federal court in the United States. The Supreme Court is made up of nine judges, called justices, and its rulings are final.

tenement: an apartment building, usually in a city, that meets only minimum standards of safety, cleanliness, and comfort.

theology: the study of God and religious doctrine, especially with regard to a particular religion, such as Christianity.

Vietnam War: the war between communist North Vietnam and noncommunist South Vietnam that began in the 1950s. The United States backed South Vietnam from the outset but did not send in large numbers of troops until the mid-1960s. Following heavy losses of U.S. soldiers, segments of the American public called for an end to the war. In 1973, a ceasefire was signed and U.S. troops withdrew. In 1975, North Vietnam defeated South Vietnam.

World War I: a major war that lasted from 1914 to 1918 and involved many countries. The United States joined the war in 1917, fighting alongside Britain, France, and (briefly) Russia to defeat Germany and Austria-Hungary. By 1918, more than 450,000 black people had moved from the southern United States to the North to take wartime jobs in factories and mines.

World War II: a major war that lasted from 1939 to 1945 and involved many countries. The United States entered the war in 1941, after Japan bombed a U.S. naval base in Pearl Harbor, Hawaii. It then joined Britain, France, and Russia to defeat Germany, Japan, and their allies.

INDEX